MICHAEL

One Unfolding Story

Story

*Biblical reflections through
the Christian year*

Edited by

Paula Gooder
and
Joanna Moriarty

CANTERBURY
PRESS
Norwich

*John Hodges
2018*

© Alison Perham 2018

First published in 2018 by the Canterbury Press Norwich
Editorial office
3rd Floor, Invicta House
108–114 Golden Lane
London EC1Y 0TG, UK
www.canterburypress.co.uk

Canterbury Press is an imprint of Hymns Ancient & Modern Ltd
(a registered charity)

Hymns Ancient & Modern® is a registered trademark of Hymns
Ancient & Modern Ltd
13A Hellesdon Park Road, Norwich,
Norfolk NR6 5DR, UK

Scripture quotations are from the New Revised Standard Version of
the Bible, Anglicized Edition, copyright © 1989, 1995 by the Division
of Christian Education of the National Council of the Churches of
Christ in the USA. Used by permission. All rights reserved.

Elizabeth Jennings, 'The Annunciation', in Collected Poems,
Carcanet Press, 1986.

British Library Cataloguing in Publication data

A catalogue record for this book is available
from the British Library

978 1 78622 049 3

Typeset by Regent Typesetting
Printed and bound in Great Britain by
CPI Group (UK) Ltd

Contents

Foreword

by the Rt Revd Rachel Treweek

One of Michael's great gifts to the Church of England was his immense contribution to shaping the liturgy and enabling people to live it well to the glory of God. He was passionate about encouraging and teaching people to live the rhythm of the liturgical year and to encounter the riches of God in Christ in every season. In his deep commitment to both Word and sacrament, Michael placed strong emphasis on being attentive to God through listening to scripture and preaching it faithfully.

In the final months of Michael's life I had a conversation with him in which I promised to ensure that there would be a publication of his sermons, preached as a gift to people in the Diocese of Gloucester and further afield.

Those themes of promise and gift now have a resonance for me with this book of sermons which span the liturgical year, beginning with Advent and finishing with Christ the King.

Advent begins with a call to watch with expectant hearts as we recall the waiting of God's people for the gift of the promised Messiah, Emmanuel – God with us. And now we continue to wait for the fulfilment of God's promise that Christ the King will come again.

In each liturgical season we live our lives amid the world's brokenness and pain, longing for God's justice, healing and peace. Michael knew such longing and struggle in his own life and ministry as he followed Christ in the way of the cross, yet always carrying the hope of Easter in his heart, confident in the mysterious promise that the ascended Christ would come again.

In these sermons we are invited to journey with Michael through the Church's year. It is my hope that amid the story of our lives, they will kindle the fire of our hearts and stir us to lift our eyes to Christ the King, the one who was first lifted up in suffering on the cross and revealed God's heart of love stronger than death.

May we allow these sermons to open our eyes and ears to the signs of God's Kingdom around us and within us, and hold fast to the promise that one day all will be made new and Christ the King will come again. God's promise of reconciliation and transformation will be complete.

In his life, Michael clung firm to the promise of that gift, and our tears at his death were mingled with the joy of knowing that he is with God and Alleluia is our song.

Although I never heard Michael preach these sermons, I have heard and seen how the Holy Spirit has used his words to nurture and deepen faith in God. It has been my privilege to follow in his footsteps as Bishop of Gloucester and I pray that these sermons will enable each of us to follow further in his footsteps as pilgrims of Jesus Christ.

Rt Revd Rachel Treweek
Bishop of Gloucester

Introduction

One of the glories of preaching on the lectionary is the sense that it provides of the rhythm and cycle for the Christian year: from Advent to Christmas and onwards through Epiphany to Candlemas; from Lent to Holy Week and Easter and from there into Ascension and Pentecost; then through ordinary time to the Kingdom season – ending with Christ the King. The Christian year accompanies us through our daily lives, through the highs and the lows, the joys and the sorrows, providing rhythm, stability and hope. As we follow its cycles we are drawn again and again into the presence of the God who created and recreates us; who loves and forgives us; who nourishes and redeems us.

There is no more vivid illustration of this than the sermons in this book. You will find here sermons that span the Christian year from Advent to Christ the King. The majority were preached during Bishop Michael's time as Bishop of Gloucester (2004–14) with a few from his time as Provost, and then Dean, of Derby Cathedral (1998–2004). The Christian year is so extensive, and the variety provided in the three-year cycle of readings so great, that it was impossible to select a sermon for every set of readings. Instead we chose representative sermons that, in our view, captured and evoked the essence of the season. We have normally included just one sermon per Sunday or major festival, but for Christmas Day we included two since we simply couldn't choose between them.

You will also find scattered throughout the book sermons

for feast days not on Sundays (such as the Feast of the Blessed Virgin Mary or the Feast of Bishop Lancelot Andrewes) as well as confirmation and ordination sermons. These represent some of Michael's great passions, as also do the two sermons towards the end of the book given to the National Association of Diocesan Advisers in Women's Ministry in 2013 and the sermon given to the Retired Clergy Association in 2011. The book ends with the sermon preached by David Hoyle, Dean of Bristol Cathedral, at Michael's funeral which beautifully captured something of who Michael was and what his faith and ministry meant to him.

Those who knew Michael will hear his voice, his passions and his faith speaking powerfully from the page as they read this book as though he were still preaching today. As you read these sermons given in different places and at different times you will see why the title of this collection is so apposite. In this collection, we have sermons preached at particular times to particular people on particular passages but they all fit together in a remarkable and inspiring way. This is because they all emerge out of, reflect on and summon us back into one unfolding story – the story of Jesus Christ who lived and loved and died and rose again. This story underpinned the whole of Michael's life and ministry and he exudes it in his sermons no matter what the day or the theme.

We dedicate this collection to his memory with love, and with gratitude for a much-missed friend, mentor, and Priest.

Paula Gooder and Joanna Moriarty
St Mark's Day, 2018

First Sunday of Advent, Year C

What are to be the marks of this Advent season? Not the outward ones, they are obvious and easy – the Advent candle or calendar, in most churches the Advent wreath or crown. No, what are to be the inward, personal marks of this Advent season? In other words, what is going on, or should be going on, inside you and me as these four weeks move forward to the celebration of Christ's birth? Something should be going on, else the season is a bit of a waste and Christmas, which follows it, a bit of a sham. Advent is here in part to help us see what is at stake when we sing, as we shall at Christmas, 'Be born in us today'.

'Be born in us today.' Now there's an invitation. An invitation to God to make his home within us, a transforming influence. Easy enough to say, but in reality hard to want deep down. Advent is here to give us a chance to reflect on whether we really want it and what the cost may be.

What, then, are the marks of this Advent season? First, hope. We speak of 'the Advent hope'. It's an important Christian concept, hope, and a powerful thing. The word 'hope' has become enfeebled in our vocabulary, and perhaps we ought to substitute a stronger word to recapture the real meaning of the Advent hope. Perhaps 'expectancy'. There's a marvellous phrase in the Acts of the Apostles that one translation puts like this: 'The people were on the tiptoe of expectation.' That's the meaning of Christian hope – an almost urgent, and certainly confident, expectation. It was there in the first reading this morning, from the prophecy of Jeremiah, with all its future tenses about what the Lord will do when the days that are surely coming come:

> *I will fulfil the promise I made to the house of Israel and the house of Judah ... I will cause a righteous Branch to spring up for David; and he shall execute justice and righteousness in the land ... Judah will be saved and Jerusalem will live in safety. And this is the name by which it will be called: 'The* LORD *is our righteousness.'* (Jer. 33.14–16)

Yes, an almost urgent and certainly confident expectation. The belief that our God is a God who acts, who acted in Jesus, and who can and will act in you and me. We have grown too used to the idea that God's activity is in the past tense, that we simply recall and remember his mighty acts. But Christian hope says, 'No, he is acting now. Don't close your eyes for a single moment or you might miss some fresh outburst of his power, some new impact of the divine upon the world. Be awake! Be alert! Be expectant!' These are all Advent calls. Believe in your heart that Christ can and will be born in you, today, tomorrow, at Christmas. Have about you the urgent hope of the Christian that spills out into confident expectation. Expectancy – the first mark of Advent.

The second mark of Advent is struggle and in particular, I think, struggle to discern the word of God for us. Advent is such a biblical season as we read all the ancient prophecies of the Old Testament that seemed to prefigure the birth of the Lord and the very testing passages of the New Testament that speak of the end of the world, the second coming and the judgement seat of God:

> *There will be signs in the sun, the moon, and the stars, and on the earth distress among nations confused by the roaring of the sea and the waves ... Then they will see 'the Son of man coming in a cloud' with power and great glory.* (Luke 21.25–27)

You don't bring anything to birth, let alone the Christ-child, without a struggle. And part of the Advent struggle is to make sense of these ancient scriptures that give this season its character and inspire its hymns, for we do need to take them seriously.

How is the word of God in Scripture a source of struggle? It's a struggle in this sense: the word of God comes to us in a variety of ways. Supremely, of course, it jumps out at us from the pages of the Bible. It comes also through the tradition of the Church, and that is itself a fragile and sensitive thing, sometimes apparently contradictory, sometimes a reassuring protection from frightening innovation, sometimes a constricting straitjacket that seems to hold us back. The tradition of the Church, and discerning God's word for us in that, is struggle enough. Yet that is not all. For Scripture and tradition are not the sum total of the ways in which God seems to be speaking to us. He speaks to us also in fresh and disturbing ways in the Church of our own day. His Spirit often challenges our old assumptions and calls us to think again. Only the very frightened will fail to acknowledge that behind the wind of change that is blowing through the Church there is something of the Spirit of God.

But God also speaks to us outside the Church. He seems to be telling us things and showing us things through nature, through art, through history, through the events of our time, through our neighbours. And besides all that – Scripture, tradition, Church, world – all of which is, in a sense, outside and around us, impinging on us, there is a voice of God within, a reason, a conscience, that is often confused, sometimes at odds with the accepted view, puzzled and perplexed. A voice within and so many voices, apparently contradictory, without; and all in some measure means by which God's word may be apprehended and received. Making sense of all these is a struggle. The process of working out what God's word is for me, and means for me, involves constant struggle. The urgent expectation of this season isn't just frothy excitement, but a deeply serious searching. Struggle – the second mark of Advent.

The third mark is repentance. Advent is not a season of

repentance in quite the way that Lent is, but repentance is very much part of the Advent story and principally because of that strange and disturbing figure, the Baptist, the Forerunner, as he is also called, who comes on the scene in today's Gospel, 'proclaiming a baptism of repentance for the forgiveness of sins'.

John is an uncomfortable figure, challenging our lifestyle and our fundamental assumptions. 'Repent!' What does that mean? Not 'give up sinning', though that might be part of its meaning. But more like 'Turn right round. Look at things in a new light.' Almost 'turn yourself upside down'. That's what the people of Thessalonica said about the first Christians in their city.

These people who have been turning the world upside down have come here also ... (Acts 17.6)

And that is indeed what the Christian gospel does. It turns us upside down. And when we have finished spinning round, we go off in a new direction. And that's repentance. You can see, can't you, how repentance emerges from expectancy? Expectancy is the conviction that God will act in you and can change you. Repentance is the turning right round, the adoption of a new perspective, that that must involve. And you can see also how repentance is often the outcome of struggle. The realization, that is nearly always self-discovery at considerable cost, that the way you had seen God, or yourself, or the world, was too narrow opens you up to new pathways. You turn and go off in a new direction. That is struggle leading to repentance. 'Bear fruit worthy of repentance' is part of John's message. So repentance – a third mark of Advent.

And the fourth, response. It is the other figures, alongside John the Baptist, hovering in the background through Advent who model this fourth mark of Advent for us. One figure is Mary, whose conception the Church celebrates on Tuesday, whose annunciation by Gabriel will bring her to the fore as Christmas draws near. And Joseph too, the village carpenter of Nazareth, he is there also in the Advent shadows waiting to come forward with his response, his alertness to the possibility of God acting.

Mary and Joseph do not think of God's activity as past tense. They have about them the first mark of Advent – expectancy. In Mary and Joseph you can also see a painful searching to know the word of God for them.'How can this be?' 'What does this mean?' 'Can it really be?' 'What am I to do?' It is a costly business for them – coming to terms with the divine initiative. They have about them that second mark of Advent – struggle. But through that struggle there emerges a willingness to have their whole lifestyle turned upside down – and therein lies at least a part of what we mean by repentance. They have about them the third mark of Advent, but in them it goes further. There is a total, willing, joyful acceptance of the divine will, a resolute 'yes' to the divine invitation. Did they know then the cost, the implications, the consequences of their response? Perhaps a little; certainly not completely. But that is the meaning of the Christian response, a 'yes' to God, an openness, a willingness, a resolution, sometimes without seeing the consequences, sometimes seeing the consequences all too well. That is the fourth mark of Advent – response; joyful, resolute response. 'I am the Lord's servant. As you have said, so be it'; 'My soul proclaims the greatness of the Lord and my spirit rejoices.'

Four marks of the Advent season – expectancy, struggle, repentance, response. The Advent wreath has four (red/purple) candles and a white one. They have their traditional meanings. But for me they equally stand for four marks of Advent. One candle for expectancy, one for struggle, one for repentance, one for response. For only when those four are truly lighted in our hearts, only when those four marks are truly part of our character, can the white candle of the presence of the Christ-child be truly alight. Without the expectancy, without the struggle, without the repentance, without the response, 'Be born in us today' will be at best a pious dream. Let this Advent so touch you that it may be something more.

First Sunday of Advent, Year A

It is the First Sunday of Advent, with its distinctive hymns, its wreath with its candles, the first one now alight, its purple vestments, its air of something different, something solemn yet joyful – just around the corner. It inaugurates one of those very subtle seasons, where things go on at different levels, and it is easy to miss the deeper levels altogether.

Advent is about coming. It is, for most, about the coming of Christmas; Advent is a sort of religious dimension to the frantic preparations to be ready for 25 December. As Christians, we might prefer to say not so much that Advent is about the coming of Christmas, but about the coming of Christ, for we recognize that part of what we are trying to do is to enter sufficiently into the mystery of the incarnation that, in a sense, Christ is born all over again, that he really comes and makes his home within us. 'Be born in us today,' we shall sing, and they won't be empty words, but a real longing for Christ to find his home within us.

And yet, of course, at another level, Advent is not about that coming at all, long ago, or even made present in us now, but about a future coming, a coming at the end of time, to judge the world, to bring all things to their appointed end. The Advent hymns we love to sing are nearly all about *that* coming, on the clouds of heaven, the sort of end-of-time events that Matthew describes:

Then two will be in the field; one will be taken, and one will be left. Two women will be grinding meal together; one will

*be taken and one will be left. Keep awake therefore, for you
do not know on what day your Lord is coming … for the Son
of Man is coming at an unexpected hour.* (Matt. 24.40–44)

Of course, the truth is that this season of comings, this Advent
time, is often squeezed out by other preoccupations. Pre-
Christmas preparation and even festivity can mean that the
Advent themes have little chance to make their impact. And isn't
the truth that we are sometimes happy enough to see Advent
squeezed out and its themes neglected? Not because we enjoy
getting into Christmas long before 25 December, but because the
traditional Advent imagery – the end of the world, the coming
of Christ to judge, the final consummation – make little sense to
us. Do we really expect these things to happen? If we can make
sense at all of 'Christ will come again' language, is it not only by
investing it with meaning very different from its plain original
sense? Isn't the second coming a bit of an embarrassment? And
the Advent hymns, with their constant invitation to the Lord to
return: is that an invitation we expect to be answered?

Here is an area of real theological perplexity for us. It is
very clear that the Lord himself lived on this earth with a belief
that the end of time was near. For him, especially as Matthew
and Mark portray him, theology was eschatology or, putting
it more simply, to talk of God was to talk of the imminent
coming kingdom. He saw his own life and death as part of a
final struggle. The disciples must keep awake, must 'be ready',
lest they be unprepared when the end came. He was wrong.
Trapped to some extent in the thought forms of his day, he was
wrong, at least about the timescale of the end.

Nor was this belief of his, that comes out so clearly in his
teaching, among the more peripheral parts of his message. The
parousia, to use the technical word, the second coming, was
central to his thinking. It shaped all sorts of his attitudes and
teachings. It was, if you like, a central plank of his theology.

And, of course, it wasn't just Jesus. The first Christians
shared this view that the end was near. They had no long-term

strategy for mission to the world, for the world was perishing. They had an immediate urgent message for a world that was passing away. The apostle Paul shared this view. Indeed his advice and teaching about ethical matters was based on the assumption that they were living in the last times. His earliest letters have a great urgency about them. The later ones begin to recognize a different time-scale before the end. And this morning, in his letter to the Romans, we read:

> ... *you know what time it is, how it is now the moment for you to wake from sleep. For salvation is nearer to us now than when we became believers* ... (Rom. 13.11)

Our Christian forebears learnt to modify the New Testament picture as each generation succeeded another and the end did not come. Nevertheless, however long delayed, the day of reckoning would surely come, and our medieval churches, in their paintings, proclaimed more than anything else the final judgement, and the division of the sheep and the goats, the saved and the damned. This emphasis on the end has been an important strand of our Christian tradition.

But what of today? Do Christians believe, do you and I believe, that God will intervene to bring the created order to an end? And, even if we do, do we seriously allow for the possibility that that intervention might come at any moment? If we do speak of a cataclysmic end, is it not one brought about by the human race in its foolishness, through weapons of mass destruction or environmental folly, rather than divine intervention, that we envisage? And, if we can envisage it, do we not fear it, rather than yearn for it, look forward to it, as the first Christians did? What do we make of those who walk up and down with their sandwich boards proclaiming a message about the end, a message that is usually taken from the Scriptures, Scripture to which we subscribe, Scripture that we read here in the liturgy through the weeks of Advent? Are we not embarrassed by those who take the Scriptures with the utmost seriousness?

I live with this dilemma. I cannot entirely make sense of the end-of-time language of the New Testament. It makes me uncomfortable. I don't quite know what I mean when I say that 'Christ will come again'. I certainly cannot picture it. Yet I am unhappy with attempts to reinterpret such language out of existence. I would fight hard against anyone trying to abandon this eschatology. I would rather cling on to these concepts of which I cannot entirely make sense than try to envisage a Christianity without them. Yes, I need to go on saying, like the first Christians in their Aramaic acclamation that John includes in his Revelation: *Maranatha*, 'The Lord is coming.'

That isn't just because such belief is central to Scripture, though it is – and that alone means that we need to take it very seriously. Nor is it only because such a belief is central to Jesus' thinking, though I don't see how you can begin to understand Jesus without taking on board something that motivated him so profoundly. Nor, in the end, is it because a faith that had jettisoned the second coming and the final judgement might be a more comfortable and cosy religion, without much guts – though that is an important consideration – for a Christianity without the judgement seat of Christ loses a proper corrective to the picture of an all-embracing love upon the cross.

No, in the end, I believe we must go on expressing our faith through the language of second coming, of judgement, of the end of time, because it is the only language we have:

- to enshrine and protect an important truth, and
- to give urgency to our proclamation.

First the truth it enshrines and protects: the language of the second coming and the end of the world enshrines and protects the social character of salvation. The Scriptures have little interest in you or me finding salvation, reaching perfection, being drawn into heaven (express it how you will) on our own. They attach little importance to the moment of death and certainly don't identify it with the time of judgement. I've always treasured a simple little truth in one of Michel Quoist's prayers: 'I cannot save myself alone.' There's something crucial there. My salvation, my perfection, my endless joy and felicity, cannot be in isolation from everybody else's. And all that end-of-the-world talk addresses that. It affirms that God wants to bring everything together, to put in the last pieces of the jigsaw, to complete the grand design, to put everybody and everything in its proper place. It is a picture in which I fulfil my eternal destiny in solidarity with all my brothers and sisters. It is a final consummation, in which all shall be well, for the elect of God.

I'm not doubting that there is a personal element to it. To some extent, I have to stand alone and face my Creator and my Saviour, but not as some private and individual encounter, but because he is bringing everything to completion and to wholeness. An event in which the totality of human history is brought to the throne of God demands strong, poetic, cosmic images, and the language of eschatology, of the second coming, of the end of time, meets that need. So, yes, *Maranatha*, the Lord is coming. Yes, come, Lord Jesus, and touch the whole world.

And then there's the concern about urgency. One of the things that followed from a belief that the end was near – it comes in the middle of the night like a thief at any moment – was a marvellous urgency to proclaim the good news, to draw men and women into the kingdom while there was still time. Yet we act, individually and as the Church, as if we had all the time in the world, and I suppose we think we have. The Church grew, the faith spread, while Christians believed the end was round the corner. The Church stopped growing, the faith weakened, when there was always tomorrow to spread the gospel. Perhaps we can recover in Advent that divine urgency that marked the whirlwind ministry of Christ, that irrepressible need to tell, that characterized the early Church. I want to hear Christ saying, 'I am coming quickly, I am coming soon', not because I can predict from that when the end will come – as if I could begin to understand the mystery of time in relation to God's eternity – but because I want to be encouraged to be urgent in my proclamation of the gospel. I want to have reinforced for me the challenge to preach the good news, in season and out of season, persuasively, joyfully, longingly, but urgently, as if there were no tomorrow. Because when we preach it like that, it will be heard. So, yes, *Maranatha*, the Lord is coming. Soon, quickly, come, Lord Jesus.

That does not alter the fact that I puzzle still over language that falls strangely on my ears. It does not remove my dilemma. It does not enable me to picture a second coming in a way that goes beyond poetry. I still have to struggle for the meaning. But I want to celebrate the social dimension to salvation and I want there to be urgency in my faith and in my proclamation.

And so on this First Sunday of Advent I say with passion and longing, with integrity and faith, *Maranatha*. Come, Lord Jesus. And I go on wrestling with words and concepts I know are too important to lose.

Maranatha. Come, Lord Jesus.

Christmas Morning I

The Word became flesh and lived among us. (John 1.14)

Where shall we put the Christmas tree? It's not a question most of you will have asked. You always put it in the same place. And the cards. And the mistletoe. It's one of the attractions of Christmas, some things at least the way they always have been. Not so, however, if you move house as my family and I have done. Christmas decorations have to be re-thought.

Where shall we put the tree? And, more importantly, where shall we put the crib? Just for a moment, till theological sense prevailed, there was a dilemma. Bishopscourt has a chapel. It is a lovely peaceful and, I think, rather holy space. Shall we put the crib in the chapel? After all, we put the crib in churches? Or shall we put it out in the hall, where people come and go, in among the Christmas decorations, in the sometimes any-thing-but-peaceful part of the house? Where shall we put the crib? Answer: out in the hall, mixed in with the festivities – visible to family, people who come to visit, people who come to stay, party-goer, meter-reader and the plumber who comes to sort out the leaking radiator. For the crib tells the story of the God who, in Jesus Christ, left the holy, peaceful space of heaven to live in a world of festivity, family and leaking radiators and things more sad and serious.

There are parallel questions. Where shall the Christ be born? Shall he be born in a palace? He comes of David's royal line. He is a prince, albeit a prince of peace. One day he will wear a crown, though one of thorns. He will claim a kingdom and people will call him Lord and Priest and King. Certainly that's where the magi from the East expected to find him. Or shall he be born somewhere that will signal something very different? Yes, he shall be born in a stable, within earshot of revellers, in sight of animals, at the end of a long journey, with no cot but a manger; the stable but a staging post on the refugee road into exile. For the stable proclaims that this baby, for all his royal blood, chooses to be one of the poor ones, one of the dispossessed, one of the marginalized. Where shall the Christ be born? In the stable he shall be born.

Where shall the news be told? Given that the *Bethlehem Citizen* was not an option, where shall the news be told? Shall it be in the temple? Old Zechariah, with his powers of speech restored now John the Baptist is born, could announce it to the people there. After all, this Jesus is their Christ, their Anointed One, their Messiah. High priests and pharisees – even sadducees – they should hear first, surely, for this baby fulfils all that the prophets foretold. He is to be a high priest whose sacrifice will save not only the nation, but the world. Shall it be the temple then? Or is there a more appropriate place? In the workplace, perhaps. Not the temple, the God-place, but in the workplace. Let it be told where ordinary people gather, honest working men, about their business, earning their living, trying to make sense of the world they inhabit. Maybe not the revellers in the inn, probably too drunk to hear the message. But who's at work at night? Why, shepherds in the field, keeping watch over their flocks by night. Let them hear the message to signify that this baby comes to bring hope and peace to them, more than to high priests and pharisees. The baby is born poor to be the poor man's friend.

In the chapel or in the hallway? In the palace or in the stable? In the temple or in the workplace? There are other contemporary questions. Where shall the Eucharist be celebrated, asked the Cathedral Chapter? In the quire, safe and secure, shutting out the tourist who might not want to be caught up in a Christian liturgy? In the quire, with its intimacy, with its echoes of a thousand years of worship and praise from monks and priests and choristers at their daily prayer? Or in the nave, open to the world, a place where people may peer around the columns and taste the liturgy from a distance, a place where no one can claim a seat as their own, the nave so often full of noisy children or chattering concert-goers, the nave where the service might be interrupted, the nave sometimes the place where lost souls sit and wonder? If it is the faith of the incarnation that we want to proclaim, God with us (not God with the Church, God with the world he loves so much), it is the market place of the nave. So the Chapter resolved.

In the hallway. In the stable. In the workplace. In the nave. Why? Because the incarnation is the place of meeting, the place of encounter, of God with his people. And it is to be an extension of the incarnation for which the Church exists – to be the place of encounter of God with his people.

'The place of encounter'. What the Church encounters in the incarnation is a God who inhabits the world in all its messiness. He is a God who inhabits a world of refugees, of tyrants, of drunken revellers, of injustices. There was blood in the stable when Mary bore the Christ and there was blood on the ground when she helped lift him down from the cross. And this Christ from birth to death was God. And what a God! A God of risks and a God of vulnerability. And the kind of Church that God rejoices in is the community with ragged edges, misfit members and all sorts of people who would never be able to belong anywhere else. The Church doesn't always cope. The temptation is to withdraw into the holy huddle, into the chapel, into the quire, into the temple. I suppose, for a bishop, into the palace! But 'God so loved the world that he sent his Son' and the Son seemed at home in the hallway, in the stable, in the workplace, in the market.

But the message of Christmas Day is not just for the Church. There is a message for our society. For in the birth of Jesus, with its talk of virgin birth, of angels and of stars, people may encounter a God who, though he does find a home among ordinary people and share their lives, however humdrum, and their relationships, however complex, nevertheless inhabits also another sphere. This sphere of the angels is a sphere of beauty, of holiness, of fragility and of love. He is God unsullied by ugliness, by profanity, by power and its abuse, by selfishness, hate and greed. He is a God who affirms who we are, sons and daughters, loves us for who we are, yearns for us to be what we could become. He is God who wants us to discover the depth of our being, our capacity for love, our potential for living to the full. He wants us to be whole, healed, reconciled, alive with every fibre of our body and every longing of our soul, in touch with heaven.

And that is what people are wanting – to be whole, healed, reconciled, fully alive. Sometimes they even take one of our Christian words to express it. 'Searching for spirituality', they say, and that is almost 'in touch with heaven'. Yet they don't look to the Church to help them find it. And that is sad, for we have an immensely rich tradition of spirituality, developed over 2,000 years. And we have ways in to spirituality through worship, through spiritual discipline, through art, through music, through Alpha Groups and much more. Have you noticed the revival of interest in angels outside the Church? But the angels belong to us, they are part of our tradition, and they are transparent ethereal beings so that God shines through them.

Yet even when looking for angels, people do not yet look to the Church, except perhaps at Christmas. For just a while at Christmas they may catch sight of the hosts of heaven singing 'Glory to God and peace on earth' and they may gaze for a while at the child in the manger who is the one who can connect them with God. In the vulnerable baby, they may catch a glimpse of the divine, an inkling of truth.

And what is that truth? Don't take it for granted. Don't assume people know it. Say it. Say it on your Christmas cards. Say it by a crib in your home. Say it whenever and however you can. This is how I've said it in my Christmas card this year, using the words of the fifth-century Caelius Sedulius:

From east to west, from shore to shore,
let every heart rejoice and sing
of Christ, the child whom Mary bore,
our Saviour and eternal King.

Now see, the world's creator wears
the very form to us he gave;
our flesh and blood the maker shares,
his fallen human race to save.

He shrank not from the oxen's stall,
he lay within the manger-bed;
and he, whose bounty feeds us all,
at Mary's breast himself is fed.

This is the truth that ought to transform the Church and change our society. Mysteriously, wonderfully, but entirely consistently with a risk-taking, self-emptying God, in the baby from Mary's womb was hidden the Maker and Sustainer of the world himself.

We may say it with some reticence to those whose experience of life has not enabled them to find this vulnerable God. We may say it with some humility in a world where Christians have much to repent of in terms of our implication in religious intolerance, racial prejudice, unjust trade practices and ineffective mission. We may say it with some sensitivity to good people of other faiths who share our reverence for the Creator and who maybe honour Jesus, but not as the only-begotten Son of the Father. Yes, reticence, humility, sensitivity all have their place in our proclamation in the modern world. But say it nevertheless we must. Proclaim it we must. Our Christian tradition teaches us and our Christian experience confirms for us that in the baby from Mary's womb we find God, God enfleshed, God incarnate, God with us:

The Word became flesh and lived among us. (John 1.14)

Hidden in the baby in the stable as surely as he is hidden in the bread of this Christ Mass:

> *God from God, Light from Light, true God from true God ...*
> *for us and for our salvation he came down from heaven: by*
> *the power of the Holy Spirit, he became incarnate from the*
> *Virgin Mary, and was made man.* (Nicene Creed)

You've heard it all before. You've maybe said it every week for 50 years as I have. But it is the truth as we have received it and we need to say it, sing it, expound it, unwrap it for a world for whom it would be a wonderful surprise, because the stable is the place of encounter:

- The Church encounters in the new-born baby, worshipped by shepherds, a God who inhabits a messy world.
- The world encounters in the new-born baby, heralded by angels, a God who inhabits a spiritual sphere that gives meaning, healing and life.

The stable is the place of encounter, and so must a cathedral be.

And, by the way, we had a friend who came to stay last week and bought us a second set of crib figures. So they are there in the chapel too! God in the messy world and God in the holy space as well.

A Happy Christmas to you all.

Christmas Morning II

Gloria in excelsis Deo and in terra pax.
Glory to God in the highest and on earth peace.

Next door, back at Bishopscourt later today there will be one of those family rituals. This one goes back about 20 years. I guess most of you have some Christmas rituals. Ours is fairly harmless, though some would think it eccentric. Once we are gathered at the dining table, at the point when (especially in a bishop's house) you might expect us to say some conventional grace, truly thankful for what we are about to receive, instead we burst into song (teenage members of the family slightly self-consciously) and what we sing is the first verse of 'Ding, dong, merrily on high'.

There was a year when we sang something different. We had to sing 'Christians, awake, salute the happy morn', but that was just that year because the precentor (in another cathedral) had failed to include it in the Christmas morning service.

But normally, it's 'Ding, dong, merrily on high'. The chorus, of course, can become a little riotous. 'Gloria in excelsis Deo' as you don't often hear it sung by the choir of Gloucester Cathedral. But that's what we sing – will sing – 'Gloria in excelsis Deo', 'Glory to God in the highest'. And it is, of course, what the choir does sing, week in week out, Advent and Lent excluded, to a host of musical settings. This morning it was Mozart. 'Gloria in excelsis Deo ... Glory to God in the highest'. So often, in fact, we sing it, or hear it sung, or say it, that we probably take it for granted. Brothers and sisters, do not take it for granted today. It is one of the catchphrases of faith. They are stupendous words. 'Glory to God.'

There seems to have been more talk this year in public debate, in the media, even among the politicians, about religion. Religion, which a lot of people have simply ignored for years, is suddenly newsworthy. Not the Church, which has always been newsworthy, as long as it is a story about some vicar falling from grace, though hardly ever when it is a story of growing church attendances. No, it is talk of religion, and its place in society. I'm not myself convinced that headlines about Muslim veils, Sikh turbans or Christian crosses greatly help the cause of religious tolerance or do much to sustain religious values. I do slightly fear that, if we overplay a campaign to assert our Christian heritage in somewhat strident tones, we may in fact play into the hands of the secularists and see that heritage eroded further. Yes, I guess it is good that people are talking more about religion. But what I really want them to do is to talk more about God.

The danger in our society is not the marginalization of religion, but the forgetting about God. And it is all the easier for that to happen because, as a society, we are so reticent to speak of him. We cringe a little when we hear the American president [George Bush] drawing God into his speeches. Our own Prime Minister [Tony Blair] was famously advised that 'we don't do God'. We do need to do God and we need to do so with openness, confidence and a lack of self-consciousness. Much more than whether people should be allowed to wear crosses on their uniform, we need to explore faith. We need to play such a role in our society that people know who it is who hung upon the cross, why he did it, and what it might mean for the wearer and for the world. We must not be content with being the 'faith communities', a collection of groups with rather odd beliefs who are nevertheless approved of because they are good at community cohesion, social action and successful schools. We must be the people who talk about God and get *other* people talking about God. We must be the people who counter the cynical dismissal of the claims of religion. We must be the people confident in the reasonableness of our faith.

Talk about God, yes, but the angels in the Gospel reading, and the choir each Sunday, and the people around the dining table this afternoon, sing '*Glory* to God'. Talk turns into praise. The angels tell us that glory is due to God, and they give that glory in their singing and they invite us to sing in harmony with them. On Christmas Day, on every day – even in Advent and Lent, even on Good Friday – to give glory to God, to be so animated by God, so passionate for God, that our approach to God is framed by worship, communion and praise.

But prior to our giving of glory is something even more significant. It is that God reveals his glory. Our giving of glory is simply a response to the divine initiative that shows us glory. What gives us a passion for God is his passion for us, his passion that we shall live life abundantly, that we shall share the loving of the Trinity, that we shall embrace the salvation he offers us. His passion for us is wonderfully expressed in that famous verse in John chapter 3:

> For God so loved the world that he gave his only Son, so that everyone who believes in him may not perish but may have eternal life. (John 3.16)

Again, like the song of angels, it can be so familiar that we do not pause to reflect on its stupendous affirmation. God so loved the world, had such a passion for its redemption, that he gave his only Son. And the giving was a revealing of his glory. For what he gave was himself, gave himself to enter our world, to be born of a woman, to be clothed in our flesh, and to walk the path of human existence all the way to the cross where he gave himself in a deeper way still. And Paul says in the Letter to Titus:

> ... we wait for the blessed hope and the manifestation of the glory of our great God and Saviour, Jesus Christ. (Titus 2.13)

And there's something crucial there. For it speaks of revealing the glory of God and it adds that that God is our Saviour Jesus Christ. God reveals his glory, but, in the end, not in creation, for all its beauty, not in miracles and acts of power, for all their wonder, not in the teachings of the wise and the holy, for all their insight, but in Jesus, a Jesus whom on this Christmas Day we picture as a little baby in a bed of straw. That's where we see the glory of God. And that, of course, is a crucial Christian perception. It's why all religions are not the same. It's what Christians want to offer, with gentle conviction, to people of other faiths. And it's what we want to offer to a world that needs a picture if it is to make sense of this talk of God.

The little baby in the bed of straw is the glory *of* God. And our response is glory *to* God. Glory to God through our joy. Glory to God through our collaboration. Glory to God through our testimony. Glory to God through our worship.

Giving glory to God through our joy, which is never a superficial jollity, but always a deep sense of delight in what God has done for us and for the world, a joy that long outlasts the tidings of Christmas comfort and joy that get put away on Twelfth Night, ours a joy that goes with us through the year, sustaining us even when the going is tough. Joy like the Epiphany wise men whom the Scriptures say were 'overwhelmed with joy'.

Giving glory to God through our collaboration. Like the Virgin Mary, with her 'yes' to God's invitation, an acceptance that changed the world. People talk of her obedience, and obedience it was, for God knew what he wanted, knew what was needed. But the response of Mary at the annunciation doesn't sound like resigned obedience, but a joyful collaborative 'yes'. And her 'yes' gave glory to God, and her seeing through of her vocation from the stable at Christmas to the cross on Good Friday and on to the upper room at Pentecost gave glory to God. And it's the same with you and me, our 'yes' to what he calls us to and our sticking with our vocation is collaboration that gives glory to God.

Giving glory to God through our testimony.

[The shepherds] went with haste and found Mary and Joseph, and the child lying in the manger. When they saw this, they made known what had been told them about this child; and all who heard it were amazed at what the shepherds told them. (Luke 2.16–18)

We are right at the beginning of the Christian story. The baby is not a day old, yet the first evangelists have set to work. The shepherds find their voice, tell the good news, pass it on, it bubbles out of them with such enthusiasm, joy, passion, that everyone was amazed. They made known God's glory and gave him glory through their testimony.

And they didn't stop there. Luke goes on

The shepherds returned, glorifying and praising God ...
(Luke 2.20)

They glorified God by their worship, by their praises. So with us. Giving glory to God through our worship. Angels do it ceaselessly. Shepherds did it as they danced through the night with good news to share. Cathedral choirs do it day in day out. Bishops do it at the dining table at least on Christmas Day. Will you do it every day – respond to the glory *of* God by giving glory *to* God by your prayers and praises?

Talk about God.
Respond to the glory of God in our Saviour Jesus Christ.
Give glory to God through your joy.
Give glory to God through your collaboration.
Give glory to God through your testimony.
Give glory to God through your worship.

It's significant that people in our half-believing society latch on to the second part of what the angels sang – the peace on earth and the goodwill to 'men'. But all the evidence is that that is just wishful thinking, and hollow wishful thinking at that, until there has been glory to God, the priority of the angels, the priority our society needs to recover.

Glory to God in the highest.
Gloria in excelsis Deo.

And a Happy Christmas to you all.

Feast of the Epiphany

Epiphany is a great day. It moves us on from the 12 days of Christmas, celebrating the baby in the manger, to a season till Candlemas when we can explore how that baby grew into a man who revealed in himself the glory of God, not least when he entered the waters of the Jordan to be baptized by John and when at the wedding feast he turned water into wine. But before that we have the story that belongs especially to this first day of Epiphany, the arrival of the magi – the word can mean wise man or magician, but not king – from the East to worship the Christ-child and to offer their gifts. Only Matthew, among the evangelists, tells the story. For him it is crucially important in revealing that Jesus was rejected by his own Jewish people, represented by King Herod, but is accepted, worshipped, by the Gentile world, represented by these kingly men from the East. Christ, he is saying, is for the Gentiles. We might want to express it a little differently: Christ is for the whole world.

You might, of course, think of today as the Feast of Jesus the Toddler. Jesus the baby at Christmas. Jesus the young man when we celebrate his baptism next week. Today Jesus the Toddler. It is a slightly facetious thought, but these wise men tell Herod that the star appeared in the East a long while ago, which is why Herod later orders the death of all the male children under two and it is why the tradition sometimes pictures the arrival of the magi as being after a journey not of 12 days, but of a year and 12 days. And that would give us not the sleeping infant in Mary's arms that most of the great artists have painted, but one who was probably walking and just about talking. And one wonders what the magi made of that and indeed what *he* made of gold, frankincense and myrrh. Christ the Toddler is a good reminder that this Jesus stays a baby no longer than any other. All too soon he grows in wisdom and stature through adolescence to manhood, when those wise men's gifts – signifying king, priest and dying man – find their fulfilment as he hangs upon the cross.

I want to think this morning about what it is that the men from the East actually do. As Matthew tells it, following the star, they set out (more than once), they rejoice greatly, they worship and they offer gifts. And there seems to be there a pattern for us to emulate as we celebrate this feast of the Epiphany. No, more than that, a pattern that is fundamental to the Christian life. Following Jesus, our light, our star, we set out (more than once), we rejoice greatly, we worship and we offer gifts.

Let's look at each in turn briefly:

After Jesus was born in Bethlehem of Judea, wise men from the East came to Jerusalem ... Then [Herod] sent them to Bethlehem, saying, 'Go and search diligently for the child; and when you have found him, bring me word ... When they had heard the king, they set out; and there, ahead of them went the star that they had seen at its rising, until it stopped over the place where the child was ... And having been warned in a dream not to return to Herod, they left for their own country by another road. (Matt. 2.1–12)

Here are men on the move. They don't so much see a light in the sky to inspire them or fascinate them or protect them, they see a light to guide them on a journey. The journey was complex, but the guidance went on, the star to get them to Bethlehem, the dream to send them on their way by another road. Had they not been adventurers, travellers, pilgrims even, we might say – for the house where the child was must count as a holy place of pilgrimage – that none of the other things would have happened. They needed to set out and to keep setting out if they were to find what they were looking for.

To say that the Christian life is a journey can sound a bit of a cliché. But theirs was not a kind of inevitable bumping along through the experiences of life. It was a conscious, perhaps costly – puzzling, I guess, for their family and friends – decision to set out. Herod, who didn't get much right, at least gave them the best advice, even if for the wrong reason. 'Go and search diligently,' he said. That's a wonderful description of the Christian pilgrimage – set out, go search diligently, though not perhaps taking your treasure chest with you as they did, but looking for treasure, looking for the pearl beyond price, which is nothing less than finding yourself entirely caught up in the embrace of the God of love. And, although there can be a moment in our life when we feel we are setting out on that journey for the first time, our own experience mirrors that of the wise men. Setting out, searching diligently, is something you go on doing – always a new path to explore, always some new truth for which to search. So, yes, brothers and sisters, set out.

Set out. Rejoice greatly.

When they saw that the star had stopped, they were over-whelmed with joy. (Matt. 2.10)

The translation – 'overwhelmed with joy' – is an attempt to signify that this is no superficial feeling happy about life. It is something deep and profound. Another moment when Matthew uses the same verb is, when we move from birth to resurrection, and he says of the women, who find the tomb empty and are told by the angel that the Lord is risen, that 'they left the tomb quickly with fear and great joy'. Again it is an overwhelming moment, deep and profound.

And that kind of rejoicing, which seized the magi, is very much the mark of the Christian pilgrim. We set out, we search diligently and, with our eyes open so that we can see, we perceive wherever we go the signs of God's love and of Christ's glory. In the big events of life, in the little everyday things, in our encounters with other people, in our personal relationships, in the Scriptures, in prayer, we perceive the signs of God's love and of Christ's glory. The wise men were the ones who could see. They had seen the star at its rising and recognized the hand of God in that and now Matthew tells us that, on entering the house, 'they saw the child with Mary his mother'. And we don't want to be people who walk through life blind, failing to see the signs of God's love and of Christ's glory. We need to train ourselves to see.

And, when we do see, we shall rejoice greatly and, just occasionally, that joy will be overwhelming. Surprised by joy, overwhelmed by joy, that's the way the Christian is, though it is never a superficial joy that is blind to the suffering of the world and the pain that Christ carries. We talk about ourselves as eucharistic people and that doesn't simply mean we come to communion quite a lot, it means that a profound and joyful heartbeat of thanksgiving is what we carry through life, a joyful heartbeat of thanksgiving to God for his goodness, for his love, for the signs of glory, for Jesus his Son.

Set out. Rejoice greatly. Worship.

They saw the child with Mary his mother; and they knelt down and paid him homage. (Matt. 2.11)

Older versions say 'they fell down and worshipped him' and the word that Matthew uses, meaning knelt or paid homage or worshipped, is one he used over and over again. Those in the boat worship Jesus when he walks on the water. The women who met Jesus on the morning of the resurrection took hold of his feet and worshipped him. The disciples at the ascension, in the final verses of the Gospel, worshipped him. 'Knelt', 'paid homage', doesn't quite capture it at moments like this. They were brought to their knees by their sense of the glory of God in the face of Jesus Christ, walking on the water, bursting out of the tomb, ascending to the Father. They fell down and worshipped him, but the magi got there first when he was just a toddler.

To worship is a deep human instinct, but so often we worship the wrong things. We are swept off our feet, not by the love of God and the glory of Christ, but by power or success or money or illusion or fantasy. We pay homage to false gods. But, in the Christian pilgrimage, it is difficult to rejoice greatly, to be overwhelmed by joy, to be eucharistic people from whom pours forth thanksgiving and praise, without that turning into worship.

And worship is both what we are doing now, the people of God giving him glory, singing his praises, paying him homage, in the liturgy, and also having about us a sense of his worth and a reverence for all that he has made in every aspect of our life. The magi found themselves brought to their knees by the Christ-child in whom they, perhaps surprisingly, saw a young prince, born to be King. Like them we are brought to our knees in worship of one whom we acknowledge as Christ our King.

Set out. Rejoice greatly. Worship. Offer gifts.

Then, opening their treasure-chests, they offered him gifts of gold, frankincense, and myrrh. (Matt. 2.11)

We don't quite know what they are doing. All three gifts can be understood as gifts fit for a king. Kingship may be the one truth about this child that they were affirming. But sometimes people have seen different messages in the three gifts – gold for a king, but incense for a priest, and myrrh for a dying man. But perhaps we are wrong to focus on what precisely the gifts were or what they mean. Instead, focus simply on the fact that what completed their pilgrimage was the offering of gifts. They set out. They greatly rejoiced. They worshipped. They gave.

And so it is also in our Christian pilgrimage that our worship, our homage, leads very naturally into the offering of our gifts in God's service. They are, of course, the very gifts he has given us. Our treasure chest of gifts comes from him, gifts of his Spirit, varying according to our need and our calling. But they are entrusted to us. We are their stewards. If we are serious about our worship, we shall want to use those gifts well in the service of Christ's kingdom. And I don't know whether it is fanciful to say that the wise men offered something of themselves to the Christ-child; certainly they had been offering up something of themselves in coming on that long mysterious journey. I do know it is important in the Christian pilgrimage that we understand that what we offer to God, alongside the particular gifts and talents he has given us, is something of ourselves, our whole being if we can manage it. The carol has got it right. 'What can I give him? Give my heart.' Yes, give my gifts, give my talents, but, more profoundly, give my heart.

And then, of course, God does his usual trick and turns it all on its head. Always he turns what we offer to him into a gift for us. He does it here, week in week out, in the Eucharist, where we offer bread and wine and he gives it back, touched, transformed, into the body and blood of Christ. He gives us himself. For that is his character – the gracious, generous, gift-giving donor, who sends us out renewed, refreshed, reinvigorated for the pilgrimage. Strengthened, once again we can set out, and find ourselves once more overwhelmed by joy, drawn to worship and offering our gifts.

Of course it is not only in the Eucharist that he gives himself, though always dependably here. In so many ways he gives himself. At this season we rejoice that in the innocence and the vulnerability of the little child he reveals to us a humble God and invites us to accept that revelation of his nature as a gift that gives life and hope.

And the magi? Did they, who drew gifts out of their treasure chests, also receive? Who knows? I suspect they returned harbouring stirrings of eternity. They went home another way; nothing could be quite the same. I hope they went with a blessing in their heart.

They deserved to, for they had followed a pilgrim path and revealed it to us. They set out. They rejoiced greatly. They worshipped. They gave gifts. It's a good pattern to follow, especially when it is the Lord Jesus Christ who is both the guiding light and also the ultimate gift of the Father.

Candlemas

It is a most beautiful feast, this day that brings Christmas and Epiphany to an end after 40 days celebrating the incarnation. A beautiful feast because it is a beautiful story, subtle, profound, with many layers of meaning. I am very glad it has been rescued from being a weekday festival, acknowledged by only the most devout, to being something that Christians can explore together on a Sunday, using it as a moment to take a last look back to Christmas, pause to celebrate the particular insights of today and then turn in a new direction with Easter in our sights.

Beautiful for the lovely moment of encounter between the younger couple, Mary and Joseph, coming timidly into the temple to do what the law required, and the older couple, Simeon and Anna, full of years and wisdom and longing, everything about to reach its fulfilment. Beautiful for the memorable words that are spoken in Simeon's *Nunc Dimittis* – Christ the light to enlighten the nations and the glory of his people – and the sobering warning of the sword that will pierce his mother's soul. Beautiful for today's distinctive ceremonies – the carrying of candles, giving the day its name, because Christ is the light, and the gathering at the font, the place of baptism that stands for womb and tomb, as we let go Epiphany and look towards Lent.

Beautiful for what looks like a little Pentecost. I'd not thought about this before, but let me share it now. As you know, there are two parallel cycles in the Christian year – Advent preparing for Christmas and then a 40-day period of praise through Epiphany till Candlemas – and Lent preparing for Easter and then a 50-day period of praise through Ascension till Pentecost. Both cycles, Christmas and Easter, end with a final feast that sums it all up, wraps it up in a sense for another year. And both are feasts of the Holy Spirit. Pentecost, of course, because the Holy Spirit comes upon the disciples gathered in the upper room. But did you hear how today, Candlemas, is also something of a feast of the Holy Spirit. Mary comes, she whom the Holy Spirit has overshadowed to make her the mother of God, with Joseph into the temple, there to meet with Simeon, of whom Luke tells us that the Holy Spirit rested upon him. And why did he come into the temple at that moment? Because, we are told, he was guided by the Spirit. See how the Holy Spirit hovers over this little gathering – Mary and Joseph, Simeon and Anna, and Jesus 40 days old.

So here we are, taking our leave of Christmas and Epiphany, allowing the stories that have belonged to the last 40 days to come into our minds once more – a baby in a manger, shepherds responding to angels, wise men to a star, a young man coming to the Jordan for baptism, calling disciples, turning water into wine – and then finding ourselves brought back to that first picture of the little baby as the parents come to present him to the Lord. What ought to be our response to these stories and to the Child who grew into a Man whom we recognize as our Saviour and Lord?

I find three responses in the story itself: worshipping, offering and speaking. Just a word about each.

It's Anna, the old widow of 84, who reminds us that the proper response to all that God has done in Jesus is to worship. Luke tells us about Anna that 'she never left the temple, but worshipped there with fasting and prayer night and day and at that moment she came and began to praise God'. Responding to what God has done by worshipping is, of course, a very Epiphany sort of thing to do. It was what the wise men did when they found the child. They got down on their knees and did him homage, as Matthew puts it, even before they presented their gifts. In a way it is the only right first response to the wonderful truth that, hidden in the baby, whether in the stable with the shepherds, or the house with the wise men, or the temple with Simeon and Anna, is God himself. Worshipping is the only right response.

And Anna's story tells us that praising is part of worshipping and what a lot there is for which to praise God in the stories we have been telling through these 40 days. She also tells us that praying and fasting are part of it too and that sounds rather more demanding and perhaps gives us a bit of an agenda as we turn towards Lent, when both prayer and fasting should come higher up our agenda. So, yes, respond by worshipping.

Offering, of course, is what Mary and Joseph do. Offer and present. They brought Jesus to present him to the Lord – thus the primary name for today, the Presentation of Christ in the Temple. And 'they offered a sacrifice, according to what is stated in the law of the Lord, "a pair of turtle doves or two young pigeons"'. They presented the child. They offered the sacrifice. At a deeper level, of course, they offered themselves. From the moment Mary had responded to the angel at the annunciation and Joseph to the dream that put him in the picture, they had in a sense handed over their lives to God, offered and presented their very selves. Do you know that lovely phrase in the old Prayer Book – it is taken up in one of the Common Worship Eucharistic Prayers?

And here we offer and present unto thee, O Lord, ourselves, our souls and bodies, to be a reasonable, holy and lively sacrifice unto thee.

Mary and Joseph, as they brought the pair of turtle doves or the two young pigeons, could well have said that. They had committed themselves to that:

And here we offer and present unto thee, O Lord, ourselves, our souls and bodies, to be a reasonable, holy and lively sacrifice unto thee.

Whether they quite knew what that would mean in terms of the offering of their lives, we cannot know. But we do know if Mary had not understood the full implications before, this was the moment when old Simeon would warn her of the suffering to come:

This child is destined for the falling and the rising of many in Israel, and to be a sign that will be opposed so that the inner thoughts of many will be revealed – and a sword will pierce your own soul too. (Luke 2.34)

Our proper response to what God has done for us in Jesus, our proper response to the lovely truth of the word made flesh, is, like Mary and Joseph, to offer ourselves, our souls and bodies, even if it involves some sort of sacrifice. Candlemas over, we shall be looking a little later towards Holy Week and there we see the ultimate sacrifice, not ours, not Mary's even, but God's own sacrifice out of love for his world.

Worshipping, offering, speaking, Anna

began to praise God and to speak about the child to all who were looking for the redemption of Jerusalem. (Luke 2.38)

And Simeon, he also speaks his words of praise and of prophecy:

Master, now you are dismissing your servant in peace ...
for my eyes have seen your salvation ....
a light for revelation to the Gentiles ...
This child is destined for the falling and the rising of many ...
(Luke 2.29–34)

They spoke out, these two wise holy ones. This coming of the child, whom they recognized as the Lord's anointed, into the temple was something for which they had long waited. It will have gone very deep with them. But they do not simply ponder silently in their hearts. They tell. They speak. They proclaim. Almost, you sense, they shout the good news.

On the whole, we are not good at speaking out. We are people of faith. We are people whose lives are directed by God. We do worship and praise and pray – and maybe even fast. Certainly in our quiet way we offer our souls and bodies. But then we go silent. We fail to tell. Everything that happened that first Christmas, all those events we have heard again through Epiphany, need to be shared with a world that hardly knows the Christian story and yet yearns to hear good news. We *have* good news, a gospel to proclaim. So we need to find our voice, each of us individually, as well as every church family corporately, to speak what God has done, just as Simeon and Anna did, unable to keep it to themselves. That's what we have, good news too exciting to keep to ourselves.

Worshipping, offering, speaking. Three responses on Candlemas Day to the wonder of the incarnation. And, if you think any of that is difficult (and you might well), remember Candlemas is a Holy Spirit day. It is the Holy Spirit, deep within us, planted within us at our baptism, who can help us to worship, can give us the courage to offer our lives, can make us confident in speaking the good news. When we gather at the font, the place of baptism, remember that. The Holy Spirit can enable you to do these things: worship, offer, speak.

Ash Wednesday

First of all let me say what a joy it is for me to begin to walk with you today on the Lenten journey to the cross and the empty tomb. I pray it may be a huge spiritual blessing to us all. Is it all right, do you think, for me to say that being here is a joy? It is Lent, after all? Is joy entirely appropriate? Are you not already beginning to wear your long Lenten faces and had I not better come into line?

George Herbert, the saintly Anglican priest and poet of the seventeenth century, spoke of this season of Lent not as a fast, but as a feast. And later in this service, within the Eucharistic Prayer, we shall find ourselves praying: 'As we prepare to celebrate the Easter feast with joyful hearts and minds we bless you for your mercy.'

Joyful hearts and minds? Joyful hearts and minds in Lent? Feast? Lent a feast? Is that how you see it? More often people have seen it as a dreary dour season. They have either rather resented it and wished its 40 days over as quickly as possible. Or, just a little more positively, they have seen it as a kind of purgatory through which we need to pass because of our rebellion and sin. Dreary and dour.

But joy and feast? That strikes a different note. Perhaps the Church has gone soft. Perhaps the old disciplines – the fasting, the prayer, the abstinence, the penitence, the spiritual reading, the solemn music – of Lent are now thought inappropriate. Is that why it is joy and feast? No need to go in for this giving-up business? Leave all that behind.

I want to say that I believe that we need the fasting, the prayer, the abstinence, the penitence, the spiritual reading and the solemn music more than ever. An age where there is more food on the supermarket shelves than ever before needs to learn the wisdom of fasting. A world where we rush from one excitement to another, or one duty to another, needs space and silence that lead to prayer. A culture of indulgence needs abstinence. A society that has lost its moral certainties needs repentance.

A generation that communicates by sound-bites needs spiritual reading. A Church that celebrates a friendly accessible compassionate God needs music that pulls us up short before the majesty and the holiness of God. And a time of economic turmoil, of international instability and of fears for the planet, needs fasting, prayer, abstinence, penitence and much more in generous measure.

So is this talk of joyful heart and mind, this sense of feast, mistaken? No. The joy is not in escaping the old disciplines but in embracing them. The feast is the fast. Lent is one of those 'turn the conventions of the world upside down' kind of seasons. Praying and fasting and all the other things begin to have their effect quite quickly. Within days, let alone weeks, we can sense that we are less enslaved to the material, more in touch with the spiritual, healthier, more alive, more alert, more sensitive, more human. All that comes from the time-honoured disciplines. We begin to feel good. Feel-good factor. It's not far from feel-good factor to joyful heart and mind. But it is the disciplines that get us there. The fast itself begins to feel like a feast.

But let's go back for a moment and just look at the origins of this season. Earlier in the service I said that since the very early days Christians have observed with great devotion the time of our Lord's passion and resurrection and prepared for this by a season of penitence and fasting.

This is how it came about. There were two groups of Christians who needed a special time for intense spiritual

37

training to make them fit for Christ. One group were those to
be baptized. Baptisms were usually at Easter, the candidates
adults, the preparation long. Two years of teaching, instruction, getting them ready for the great moment when they would
go down into the water, be anointed, joined to the Church and
share in the Eucharist for the first time. And when those two
years were almost up, the candidates changed gear. Forty days
of real rigorous spiritual training for the momentous day. They
kept what we now call Lent. The other group were those who
had been excluded for a while from the sacraments because of
some serious or scandalous sin. They had been, as we would
put it, excommunicated, as a kind of penance. They were to be
readmitted to communion at Easter. They too went through
40 days of real rigorous spiritual training for the welcome day
when they returned to the eucharistic fold. They too kept what
we now call Lent. And it wasn't long before it spread. The
candidates for baptism were doing it. The penitents were doing
it. Would it not be spiritually beneficial to us all to be doing it,
people began to ask. And so it was that the holy feast or fast of
Lent became a season for the whole Church, as it is for us from
today. Lent was, of course, for those candidates and penitents,
and is for us, about the journey to the cross. It is a dynamic
season, as a season that marks a journey has to be. It is a season
on the move, a journey, a pilgrimage, keeping up with Christ as
he sets his face resolutely towards Jerusalem.

But hang on, you may say, I thought Lent was about Jesus
in the wilderness for 40 days and isn't that about as static as
you can get, stuck in the desert for six weeks? What's dynamic
about that? Here we have to sort out a confusion. Lent is not
about Jesus in the wilderness and you notice that the Gospel
for today is not that story about temptation from the devil. We
do hear that next Sunday, simply because, if we are keeping
a time of spiritual fitness training, we need some Bible stories
that engage with that to encourage us. And Jesus doing the
same is just such a story. But the Lent story is not the wilderness story, but the hillside story, the story of Jesus walking

with his cross until he comes to Calvary, though to get there we may well walk through the desert and find it a strangely purifying place to be. But the Lent invitation is not to stop in the wilderness, but to try to keep up with Jesus as he walks resolutely towards that goal. And all the way he walks, not with a glum face like one who goes to his doom, but with the joy of one who does the Father's will, who knows that the cross will become a source of life and peace, and with a lightness in his step. More feast than fast. And that is the pilgrimage which begins for us today also.

But of course there is a problem for us, though not for him. The problem is sin. How can we walk joyfully behind him, or even trap him in conversation, or tell him, in our restrained English sort of way, that we love him and would give our lives for him, when sin gets in the way? You need to understand that the principal outcome we are looking for in Lent is growth – growth in faith, growth in discipleship, growth in wisdom, growth in Christlikeness, growth in love of God and one another and, in a particular sense, of self. That is what God wants to bring about in us through the Lenten pilgrimage. Growth, more than penitence.

But penitence, lest you thought I had forgotten it, is what *today* is about. Ash Wednesday is the principal penitential day of the year. We focus hard on our sin today, not so that it may depress us or open wider the gap between God and ourselves. We focus hard on our sin today, both so that there may be real self-knowledge, self-awareness, which is the precondition to growth, and also so that we may, having identified our sin, hand it over to Christ, let go of our burden, receive forgiveness, so that, set free, we can walk with him through the desert to the cross.

At the heart of our service tonight is a silence in which we do just that. We identify our sin and we hand it over to Christ. We let him put his cross upon us once again, a sign both of *our* penitence and of *his* forgiveness. The cross will be marked again on each one of us in dust and ashes to mark our penitential entry into the Lenten feast and fast. It's not a bit of showing off to the world – Jesus warns against that. You don't have to wear that black smudge through Lent any more than you have to wear a long face. Wash it off as soon as you get home, just as Christ washes you clean of sin. It is a sign just for you, the cross traced once again upon you, to put you under starter's orders for the Lenten pilgrimage, which is more marathon than sprint through the desert to the cross. The cross is the sign of rejection, of failure, of pain, of humiliation. And yet, for the Christian, it turns out to be the sign of life and joy and peace and victory. It's another of those 'turn the conventions of the world upside down' elements of faith. The cross is joy hidden in shame. Good Friday is glory hidden in tragedy. Just as Lent is feast hidden in fast.

Feast hidden in fast. Yes, there is a need to fast. But if the ashes are the sign of the fast, equally tonight Jesus gives you the food and drink of the feast. It is a demanding journey we are going to make through Lent to Easter and we need food and drink for the journey. Sinners as we are, even today he gives us bread. Not the bread of this world's physical hunger, for Lent reminds us that we do not live on bread alone, but the bread, the sustenance, of his holy word, the word 'that proceeds from the mouth of God', and the bread also of the Eucharist, 'bread of angels' who ministered to Christ through 40 desert days. Food for the journey. The Church gives us ash, a sign of reconciliation. Christ gives us bread, the feast for those who have been reconciled, and he gives it again and again.

So, with joyful hearts and minds, let us embrace together the disciplines of this season, more feast than fast, and walk together and, before long, experience the feel-good factor once again – more alive, more alert to Christ, to his people and to the world for which he died.

Palm Sunday Homily

Deprived of our procession from the Market Place this morning, we need to use our imaginations to picture what Christians have done for many hundreds of years in many parts of the world on Palm Sunday morning and what thousands will be doing today. Some of you have heard me quote this before, but to help you imagine it close your eyes, if you will, and listen to the account of Palm Sunday in Jerusalem in the fifth century, though it would be little different today:

> *The bishop and all the people rise from their places, and start off down from the summit of the Mount of Olives. The babies and the ones too young to walk are carried on their parents' shoulders. Everyone is carrying branches, either of palm or olive, and they accompany the bishop in the very way the people did when once they went down with the Lord. They go on foot all down the mount to the city, and all through the city to the main church, but they have to go pretty gently on account of the older women and men among them who might get tired.* (Egeria, fifth century)

That's an account of Palm Sunday in Jerusalem 1,600 years ago, written in her travel diary by a nun called Egeria. People have been marking this Sunday of the Passion like that through all the centuries since. Of course, it doesn't rain much in March in Jerusalem. In reality, it doesn't rain much on Palm Sunday in England. It poured with rain in Winchester in 1984, but every year since I've taken part in an outdoor procession on Palm Sunday morning, 23 years running. But today we have had to use our imaginations.

I hope that, in our liturgy today, even with the procession reduced to just a few yards, you won't have missed two things. They are very simple.

The first is this. Jesus Christ is in our midst. We accompany him in his journey into the city as we shall on his journey out of the city on Good Friday. We accompany him. Or he accompanies us. When we walk confidently and joyfully through parts of our life, he is at our side. When we stumble, fall, pick ourselves up and struggle on, at other points in our life, he is at our side. Indeed it is he who picks us up. In the liturgy Christ is always present in our midst. He is here in the reading of the Scriptures. He is here in the bread and wine over which we give thanks and which we share. It doesn't have to be Palm Sunday for that to be true. But we sense it today particularly, the Lord, who is here in our midst, walking with us.

Second, this is a liturgy that moves us on. It starts, absolutely rightly, with the joy of a wonderful highpoint in the ministry of Jesus, one of those moments – and they were few enough – when people caught on, at least in part, to who he was and honoured him with their branches and their cloaks and their hosannas. And we want to celebrate that, to be joyful in that, and to recognize that he is for us also the one who comes in the name of the Lord. But, of course, the affirmation didn't last long on that first Palm Sunday. Had we read even a few more verses from the account of the triumphal entry, we would have heard of a Jesus locked in controversy with the authorities and dramatically turning over the tables of the money changers in the temple. The hosannas faded fast.

And, if we were to go away from here this morning simply with those hosannas echoing in our ears and let them dictate our mood till we come together again on Maundy Thursday night, we would be failing to walk with Christ. For, from the moment he arrived in the city, the walk became not a triumphal procession (or at least no ordinary one), but a walking to the cross. And so, we soon left behind the carnival atmosphere of the first Palm Sunday, laid aside our branches and have listened to Matthew's account of the Lord's passion, so that we may be truly tuned in to what he was experiencing in Holy Week. And now, very soon, we will share the broken body and the blood outpoured for the world's salvation, because it is the passion, rather than the palms, that we need to carry with us through these coming days, if we are to go deep with Christ into the mystery of his death and resurrection.

Do you remember how, in the story of the raising of Lazarus, an event just before Holy Week, Thomas says to the other disciples, 'Let us also go with him, that we may die with him'? Like Thomas the apostle, like Egeria the nun, like countless disciples down the ages, we have begun to go with him through the week of his passion. It is a good journey to make together.

Chrism Eucharist on Maundy Thursday

Come, anointing Spirit, touch my lips.
Come, Spirit of truth, illuminate our minds.
Come, Holy Spirit, Fire of love, fill our hearts.

Jesus begins to bathe your feet with his tears and continues to kiss them and to anoint them. (Luke 7.36–50, adapted)

It is an amazing story, isn't it, that Luke tells: amazing, out-rageous, sensual, not very Church of England really? Of course Luke is not the only Gospel writer to tell the story of such an anointing. There are *few* stories that *all* the evangelists tell – the feeding of a multitude, the entry into Jerusalem, the passion, the empty tomb – not much more. But they *all* tell how a woman anointed Jesus. They tell it with much variety of detail, and sometimes more than detail, but Luke's is the richest and the most outrageous. In Matthew a woman anoints the *head* of Jesus in the house of Simon the leper. The same in Mark. In John it is in the home of Lazarus, on the eve of Palm Sunday, that Mary, the sister of Lazarus and Martha, anoints the feet of Jesus only days before Jesus washes the feet of his disciples. In Luke the unnamed woman is a sinner, and again it is feet that are anointed and with tears and with kisses. Outrageous and sensual.

Jesus begins to bathe your feet with his tears and continues to kiss them and to anoint them.

What an appropriate Gospel for this morning – the one Common Worship gives us for this Chrism Eucharist one year in three. Appropriate for a diocesan gathering. Appropriate for a great gathering of the *laos*, the people of God, with their ordained and licensed ministers, with our common calling, whether we are churchwardens or priests, local ministry members or bishops, readers or diocesan officers, deacons or lay workers, each with a ministry for which I give thanks today. Appropriate for each one of us, giving thanks for one another and encouraging one another, because, for all the distinctiveness of our different callings and ministries (for which praise the Lord), there is a common message for us all to hear.

The overwhelming message of today's Gospel is this. Like the woman who anointed the Lord, love Jesus passionately and intimately. Love Jesus, passionately and intimately. Behind that, perhaps, love the God we see in Jesus passionately and intimately. And perhaps, in recognizing Jesus' acceptance and commendation of the woman whose behaviour others thought shocking, know that God loves you passionately and intimately.

Love Jesus, passionately and intimately.
Love the God we see in Jesus, passionately and intimately.
Know that God loves you, passionately and intimately.

And forget that theology about God being without passions. Ours is a passionate God of tears and kisses and generous anointings!

That's the overwhelming message, but let's unpack it a little further. First, note that the woman knows herself accepted before ever Jesus speaks. Her action in anointing his feet precedes any declaration that her sins are forgiven. Christopher Evans in his commentary on Luke suggests Jesus must have, at some earlier moment unrecorded in Scripture, have declared her sins forgiven. But, no, she does not need to hear him say 'Your sins are forgiven' before her love can flow, or before his body language, his gestures, his eyes of love, invite. She is drawn to him by who he is, given confidence by his demeanour of welcome and acceptance, released to express her love by the love that radiates from him. That's the way the love of God in Jesus is. Our reading from Revelation says just that, 'To him who loves us and freed us'. The love of Jesus invites, invites you, invites those among whom you live and minister – inviting sometimes *through* you. How our bearing conveys welcome, acceptance and the love of God can make all the difference in the world to those looking for the good news of Christ.

That's the first thing. She knows herself accepted before ever Jesus speaks. Second, she knows that her failure, her sin and her brokenness do not get in the way. Like the woman at the well in the Gospel earlier in Lent and like the woman caught in adultery, she discovers that failure, sin and brokenness do not get in the way of the love of Jesus. They need dealing with. Failure needs sometimes to be accepted, sin needs to be con-fessed, brokenness needs to meet healing, but they do not get in the way of the unconditional love of Jesus. 'While we were yet sinners, Christ died for us,' as Paul says. In life, in ministry, we mess up – just sometimes, most of us, spectacularly – and like a prodigal son have to return from a far country, only to meet the God whom Jesus reveals running to meet us with out-stretched arms. But, more of the time, we have not wandered off into a distant land. We have simply fallen short, lost our vision or our energy, let things slip a bit. There is no need of a dramatic returning, simply a need to open our eyes to see Jesus at our side, his arm around us or his hand on our shoulder, assuring, understanding, encouraging, not much interested in our success, but delighting in the love, however hesitant, we have for him.

The woman knows herself accepted before ever Jesus speaks. She knows her failure, her sin and her brokenness do not get in the way. Third, she understands the power of anointing.

Turn our story on its head for a moment. In John's Gospel, of course, exactly that happens. In chapter 12 a friend anoints the feet of Jesus; in chapter 13 Jesus washes the feet of friends. So, before we look at what it means for you to anoint the feet of Jesus, think about what it means for Jesus to anoint your feet. And remember what Jesus told Peter – feet stand for the whole body. If he washes your feet, you are altogether clean. If he anoints your feet, you are *covered* in oil.

So hear again that little reversal of the story with which I began this sermon:

Jesus begins to bathe your feet with his tears and continues to kiss them and to anoint them.

'Anoint and cheer our soiled face with the abundance of thy grace', they sang when those of you who are priests were ordained, calling down the anointing Spirit. 'Anoint and cheer our soiled face with the abundance of thy grace', we will sing when those of you who are to be ordained priest kneel before this altar table in nine weeks' time. 'Anoint and cheer our soiled face with the abundance of thy grace', we shall sing in a few minutes as we bring the holy oils to be blessed this morning. Sometimes the anointing that we receive is a literal one with oil – in baptism and confirmation, in ordination, in sickness. Sometimes it is not literal, but metaphorical, but always it is anointing with the Holy Spirit and always it is with the abundance of God's grace – fabulous phrase, isn't it, 'the abundance of God's grace'?

Down on his knees, our humble Lord, ministering to those often not very beautiful parts of us, our feet, washing them, not with water from the river or even the tap, but with his tears, tears where joy, pain, forgiveness and love are all mixed in together, as they so often are in human relationships.

Washing our feet. Kissing our feet in the extraordinary intimacy of touch. It is the action of a lover. That's the kind of relationship into which we are invited. You know those

47

wonderful lines in John Newton's hymn 'How sweet the name of Jesus sounds'?

Jesus, my shepherd, husband, friend,
My prophet, priest and king!

And some hymn reviser (they're worse than liturgists, you know!) decided 'husband' wouldn't do. Perhaps too intimate, perhaps too gender specific, and he (I am sure it was a he) changed it to 'brother'. 'Jesus, my shepherd, brother, friend'. What a cop-out! Lacks the intimacy, doesn't it, feels rather safer? What he ought to have done, if 'husband' had to go, was to substitute 'lover'. That's the Jesus who caresses feet.

Jesus, my shepherd, lover, friend,
My prophet, priest and king!

And to meet that Jesus and experience the mutual giving and receiving of that love there is no substitute for time with Jesus in prayer, in exploration of Scripture, in participation in the sacraments. Without this, the love affair will not blossom.

But, to come back to the story, it is of course Mary who does the anointing. She anoints the Lord and provides us with a model to do the same. How can we anoint Jesus?

We do it, of course, through our part in the mutuality of prayer, Scripture and sacrament, the giving and receiving, the speaking and listening. We do it also by seeing Jesus in those around us and in our loving them with the love we have from him. And we do it by anointing.

We anoint Jesus in the child we anoint at baptism. I anoint Jesus in the adult I look in the eye as I mark their forehead with the cross in the holy oil at confirmation. We anoint Jesus in the people whose feet will be washed tonight. I anoint Jesus in the deacons on whose hands I will mark the cross in the oil of chrism when I ordain them as priests in July. We anoint Jesus in the suffering person looking for healing of disease or reconciliation to God. We anoint Jesus in the dying person to prepare them for heaven. Seeing Jesus, loving Jesus, in these his, our, brothers and sisters, Jesus who loves us and freed us.

This is no mechanical ritual if it is a means of grace and we the channels of that grace. Often, of course, to speak of anointing is metaphor. There is no oil, there may even be no touch, but there is ministry that is driven by love, ministry in which we see in those to whom we minister the figure of the well-beloved and well-loving Christ. And sometimes, conscious of the pitfalls, of course, and careful because of all the issues about professional boundaries and the dangers of inappropriate behaviour, there will be touch, there will be embrace, for this is ministry like that of the woman who kissed the feet of Jesus and like a Jesus who washed and dried the feet of his friends. Extraordinary intimacies!

It is all summed up for us, of course:

The one to whom little is forgiven loves little.
But she has shown great love.
(Luke 7.47, adapted)

So, renewing vows, acknowledging failure, giving thanks for the abundance of grace, looking for anointing once again, hear Jesus say to you, 'I love you. Passionately and intimately I love you.' And, in response, find the courage to say to the God we see in Jesus, 'I love you, at least a little and I would love you more.' Jesus bathes your feet with his tears, kisses them, anoints them again today.

To him who loves us and freed us from our sins by his blood,
and made us to be a kingdom, priests serving his God and
Father, to him be glory and dominion for ever and ever. Amen.
(Rev. 1.5–6)

Maundy Thursday Evening

[Jesus said] I do not call you servants any longer, because the servant does not know what the master is doing; but I have called you friends, because I have made known to you every-thing that I have heard from my Father. (John 15.15)

Those are the words of Jesus in John chapter 15. In chapter 13 he washes their feet and then he begins to teach them and it is not long before he is talking about friendship, calling them his friends. Servants no longer, but friends. And he reminds them that there is no greater love in all the world than to lay down one's life for one's friends.

Becoming God's friend is something really important for a disciple of Jesus Christ. St Gregory of Nyssa taught that 'the one thing truly worthwhile is becoming God's friend'. To me that is a powerful idea.

Deep human friendship is a wonderful gift, enriching our lives, a relationship in which there is trust, affection, mutuality, permission to be vulnerable, permission sometimes to be unrea-sonable and yet still be loved, a relationship that will sometimes be marked by stimulating conversation, sometimes by shared silence, sometimes by an embrace, most often by simply being at ease. It is something like that that Jesus offers us when he says, 'You are my friends'. It is something like that that God looks for when he yearns for us to become God's friend.

So, tonight, Jesus gathers with his disciples in an upper room, and there he takes the towel and the bowl and the water and moves among them washing their feet. Now the washing of feet in the communities of Jesus' day was the task of the slave and, because of that, when we reflect on this story we sometimes speak of it as an act of service. It may lead us indeed to talk about Jesus modelling servant leadership; I've often used it that way myself. But it has never seemed to me that service is quite what Jesus is modelling here as he kneels among his disciples.

Or sometimes (and this is getting nearer the truth), we see it as modelling humility. After all, this master on his knees is the Lord of heaven and earth, this is God incarnate who is washing their feet. I've always liked that reversal of roles from Bethlehem to Jerusalem. In Bethlehem at Christmas the working men, the shepherds, get down on their knees to the new-born Christ. In Jerusalem at Easter it is the Christ, as he moves to his passion, who gets down on his knees to the working men, the tax collector and the fishermen. So, yes, there is some modelling of humility here. But it doesn't get quite to the heart of what he is doing.

The heart of it is that what he models is love, because he has taken the task away from the slave, not in order to be the slave, but to show that this is a task for a friend. Jesus does this because of friendship and then helps them to see its meaning when he talks at length with them in what we call the farewell discourse in the following chapters of John, where he calls them friends and helps them to see that their relationship is not about servanthood, but about friendship:

> *[Jesus said], I do not call you servants any longer, because the servant does not know what the master is doing; but I have called you friends ...* (John 15.15)

A wise deacon, Robert, in our partner diocese of El Camino Real, has helped me to deepen my understanding of this. And a deacon, of course, is just the person to do so, for the word we usually translate as servant is the Greek *diakonia*, deacon. Robert explains that essential to understanding *diakonia* in a

Christian context is the recognition that these kinds of activities in Greek cannot involve the services of a slave or hired hand. The performance is always done by a family member, a social equal or a friend.

Illustrative of this is the marriage feast at Cana, another of John's stories. The *diakonoi* who are in charge of the wine are not servants or slaves. They are the best friends of the bridegroom, performing a similar service as groomsmen and bridesmaids in weddings today, where no one is under the illusion that they are servants or slaves. So here in the washing of feet, Jesus is saying, in effect, this kind of ministering is not a task for a slave, but for a friend, and I am your friend. It is an act of love.

And I don't think I quite know what to make of Peter's reluctance. Is it because he hasn't understood and thinks Jesus is inappropriately playing the slave? Or is it that he understands only too well that this is Jesus offering friendship with all its openness, its vulnerability and its affection and he is not quite sure he is ready for such a relationship? Too much intimacy in the air. Either way he soon moves on and grasps at the grace on offer – 'don't just wash my feet, but all of me'.

Jesus wants you to know he is your friend. Jesus offers you the intimacy of friendship. Jesus yearns for you to be God's friend. In the washing of feet tonight he is saying that to you. 'I am your friend. I offer you the intimacy of friendship. Become, or become more deeply, God's friend.'

And then comes the supper, which John assumes and Paul describes. Jesus, as one of our Eucharistic Prayers puts it, 'comes to table with his friends'. He's washed their feet, he's beginning to talk about friendship. This is a love feast. It's the meal shared by intimates where profound things can be said and communion experienced. I love the Eucharist. So do you or you wouldn't be here. I love its mystery. I love its wonder. They bring me to my knees. 'Therefore we before him bending this great sacrament revere.' That's really important to me, venerating Christ in the Eucharist, recalling with awe the sacrifice of Calvary, handling the holy gifts with reverence, all those truths our Catholic forebears taught us. But I also want to recapture the sense of the Eucharist as the love feast, as a meal with Christ and with his friends, with the intimacy of the eyes that meet across the table, with the affection of those who readily embrace one another, sensing the arms of God around them. Every Eucharist a coming to table with his friends.

Jesus wants you to know he is your friend. Jesus offers you the intimacy of friendship. Jesus yearns for you to be God's friend. In the sharing of the supper tonight, in the giving of his body and his blood, he is saying that to you. 'I am your friend. I offer you the intimacy of friendship. Become, or become more deeply, God's friend.'

And so with Jesus we go out into the night, into the dark. For a while we may show that we are his friend, that we love him, by keeping watch as if in Gethsemane. It's there that we see how our vulnerable Lord needed the friendship of those who were close to him – Peter, James and John. How he needed them then. But there we see the failure of friends. They sleep when he needs them most to be awake and at prayer. And later, when he is led away, we see the desertion of friends, as they flee, scatter, deny even, all of them save John, Beloved Friend, who is there next day at the foot of the cross with the stoical women. But that is a story for tomorrow.

It may sound rather intrusive, perhaps more than you can cope with, a Jesus who desires your friendship, offers you his, looks for mutuality, cannot hide vulnerability. You can't quite know where it might lead you; it could change a lot in your life. Being servant to his master may be an easier option.

But a Jesus who desires your friendship, offers you his, looks for mutuality, cannot hide vulnerability, may seem wonderfully attractive; it may speak to the deep longing in your heart. Yes, to really know his friendship, yes, to really be God's friend, yes, that's what I need above all else and I hadn't understood it.

The scene in the garden, in the dark of the night, is sobering. For, however long you keep watch tonight, eventually you will walk away. At moments, like Peter and James and John, you will deny your friend, you will desert your friend, you will not be sure you want to be the friend of God. The cares of this world or the sense that this relationship carries too much risk of turning your world upside down will have you walk away. But even here there is good news. For Christ will take your selfishness, your fear, your heart of stone, your sin and carry it with his cross to the hill outside the city and allow himself to be nailed to that cross and, looking down from it, will say to you, as he says to me, 'No one has greater love than this, to lay down one's life for one's friends. You are my friends.' Even though you are hiding, even though you have left me alone, you are my friends.

So, in the washing of feet and in the sharing of the supper, but also in the going out into the darkness of the night, Jesus says to you, as to me, 'I am your friend. I offer you the intimacy of friendship. Become, or become more deeply, God's friend.' At every stage as the passion unfolds, hear the words of Gregory: 'The one thing truly worthwhile is becoming God's friend.'

He came from his blest throne,
Salvation to bestow;
But men made strange, and none
The longed-for Christ would know.
But oh, my Friend,
My Friend indeed,
Who at my need
His life did spend.
Here might I stay and sing,
No story so divine;
Never was love, dear King,
Never was grief like Thine.
This is my Friend,
In whose sweet praise
I all my days
Could gladly spend.
('My song is love unknown', Samuel Crossman)

Good Friday Homily

Yes, it is finished. 'It is finished' is what Jesus cries out. The ordeal is over. He has gone through it all, save death itself, and that is now to take him over. He has walked the sorrowful way with passion and yet with dignity, and it is over. It is finished.

And yet it is more than that. It is accomplished. Something has been achieved, something immeasurable, something eternal, something that changes the whole relationship of the human race to its Creator. Paul tells us that 'God was in Christ reconciling the world to himself' and, though that process begins in the stable at Bethlehem, it reaches its climax on the hill outside Jerusalem.

For John, whose account of the passion is always appointed for Good Friday, the cross is all accomplishment. It is not disaster, or failure or tragedy. It is the will of God. It is the means of the world's salvation. It is good news, gospel, for the human race. And so his account of the life and death of Jesus Christ is all about glory, but glory of a strange divine sort that the world fails to perceive. Jesus' path through human life is a triumphal procession revealing the glory of God, and the cross is the grand climax, where the ultimate victory is won. 'I, lifted up from the earth, have drawn everyone' – 'the whole world' he might have said – 'to myself.'

And this ancient liturgy of Good Friday, that had already taken on this mood and shape as early as the fourth century, has John's perspective. For all the solemnity, for all the austerity, for all the deep emotions, there is a quiet confidence and more than a hint of glory. We wait for Easter when our risen Lord will be among us, but we know that his victory does not delay till then. It is won high upon the cross, the world drawn to him, divine nature revealed, and humankind reconciled to God.

A little later you will be invited to kneel for a moment at the foot of the cross, individually and informally, or stand there if your limbs won't do what you want them to. To come to the cross, to kneel there if we can, is our natural and proper response. It is just to worship, to be thankful, to gaze at the sign of our redemption. There is nothing else we can do. Jesus has done it all, and has done it alone, has accomplished it.

Once, only once, and once for all,
His precious life he gave;
Before the cross in faith we fall
And own it strong to save.
('Once, only once, and once for all', William Bright)

But first we turn to prayer for God's world. We bring to the Lord his whole creation crying out for a redemption that is there on offer. And in that prayer from our hearts is a response to the cross that is different from a silent gazing on our knees. For in that prayer we are not so much gazing up at the cross, but with our Saviour looking down from the cross on to the world in love and pity and longing. That is what true intercession is, looking, praying, with Christ, in love and pity and longing, that all that was accomplished upon the cross may be recognized, received, accepted and lived by the men and women for whom Jesus died.

Yes, it has all been accomplished, and accomplished alone by Christ. Yet, also, he still has work to do, and this he does not do alone. The reconciliation needs to be preached, to be shared, to be lived, so that the world may believe, and come to its senses and return to the Father. This, his continuing work, he does through us. And we show our willingness, even if it be a half-hearted and feeble willingness, as we stop gazing at the cross from afar, come up to the altar, receive the broken body and precious blood, and so unite ourselves with his sacrifice, share his destiny, accept his way of suffering, and pledge ourselves to make known his salvation in all the world.

Paul says, 'Every time you eat this bread and drink this cup, you show forth his death until he comes.' And yes, on Good Friday of all days, we do show forth his death as we share the broken bread and the wine that has been poured out. But also that very bread and wine provides the spiritual nourishment to strengthen us as we proclaim his death, his reconciling love, in word and action, by the very way we live out our discipleship of the crucified and risen Lord.

And the message that comes from our receiving his body and his blood is that, in the end, we do not so much gaze at him as share with him. It has been accomplished, once for all, yet there is a mission to be fulfilled. In the fulfilling of it, there are sacrifices to be made and suffering to be shared. But there is more than a glimpse of glory.

Easter Day

Alleluia! Christ is risen.
He is risen indeed. Alleluia!
Jesus, bursting from the tomb, touch my lips.
Jesus, victorious over death, illuminate our minds.
Jesus, crucified risen glorified Lord, fill our hearts.
('Alleluia! Christ is risen', Christopher Wordsworth)

If you are a gardener, or indeed if you like looking at beautiful gardens (which is nearer the mark in my case), the last few weeks have been a time of pleasure mixed with anxiety. The pleasure has been at seeing the vibrant colour return after the winter in the blossom on the trees and even some green leaves emerging now and the flowers coming first into bud and then into bright yellows and pinks and blues – hyacinths, daffodils, tulips and more. Nature doing that apparently miraculous thing it does every year. The anxiety, of course, is whether a frost might come at the worst of moments and ruin the blossom and bring the flowers to a premature end. And frost there has indeed been this last week, not too severe, especially in the city, so perhaps it will be all right.

Gardens, of course, play a key part in the Christian story, though the Bible that almost begins in a garden ends in a city, not the old Jerusalem of the Gospels, but the new Jerusalem of the world to come, of which the Revelation to John speaks so eloquently. So there is hope for city dwellers, urban man and woman – God is not only found in the countryside!

Nevertheless, gardens are important. First there is the Garden of Eden, such a crucial element in the Genesis creation myth, a garden into which God puts first a man and then a woman, Adam and Eve, symbolically the first ancestors of humankind. God places them in a garden, not just to sit and admire the blossom and the flowers, but to till it and keep it. Adam is to be the gardener, to create with God something beautiful and delightful to enjoy. There are trees too in the garden, though there is one tree in the middle that Adam and Eve are instructed to leave well alone.

Of course it all goes wrong. They eat the fruit of the forbidden tree and the consequences are dire. Nothing less than banishment from this garden of delight, expelled, denied its beauty, driven into a barren place. Words like 'sin' and 'fall' creep into the story. Adam and Eve are disobedient to God and that's bad enough, but it may not be the worst thing. They try to hide from God, as if they could, no longer able to look God in the face, so to speak, which is worse. And that relationship with God is in tatters, and that matters most – their relationship with God has failed. And beyond that, their relationship with one another has suffered a blow too. Suddenly there is no easy intimacy between them. They find that they are naked and, even with one another, they have to hide behind fig leaves, no longer at ease in their bodies or their souls.

Don't get hung up on whether this is history. That's not what it's meant to be. It is a powerful story about alienation, separation, relationships marred and broken. The Garden of Eden, from which they are led out, and cherubim with flaming sword set on guard to keep them out, and to guard the way to the tree of life.

Now turn to another garden, this one on a hillside in Jerusalem, the garden they called Gethsemane. Jesus has shared supper with his friends, taken bread and spoken of his body to be nailed to a cross, and a cup of wine and spoken of his blood to be shed for all, and then out into the garden in the dark of the night. With him he takes Peter, John and James. He asks them to pray and then he withdraws a little from them that he too may pray to his heavenly Father. Some of this story has some echoes of Eden. There are relationships that are breaking. Judas has already disappeared into the night intent on betraying his friend. Peter is about to deny his Lord. And, even before that, these three chosen companions are about to fail the simple test of staying awake to pray. Friendship is falling apart. And out of *this* garden also people will be led – well, perhaps only one person will be led out on a journey to a barren place; only one because the others will simply flee. Alienation, separation, relationships marred and broken.

But, wait, at the heart of it there is this man on his knees, praying with such intensity that his sweat is like drops of blood, prayer that can only be called an agony, because this man, this new Adam, is trying to turn things round. 'Father, let this cup pass from me. Nevertheless not my will, but yours, be done.' This new Adam does not disobey like the one in the Garden of Eden. This new Adam is not hiding from God; he is opening himself up to God. This new Adam is perfect in his obedience to the Father's will. Here in the garden he is beginning to put things right.

Of course, he cannot complete the work here, for the path of obedience will take him along the *Via Dolorosa* and outside the city, to the barren hill, the city tip, the place of bones. There on a new tree of life he brings to perfection the work he has begun. It is costly for him, supreme sacrifice, not just because of the excruciating physical pain, but also because, at least as Mark the evangelist saw it, he goes to his death with a sense of his own relationship with God in ruins – *'Eioi, eloi, lama sabachthan?* My God, my God, why have you forsaken me?'* Perhaps so, but, with retrospect, we can with the Fourth Gospel hear instead from the cross the cry of triumph, 'It is accomplished!'

What has been accomplished? The restoration of relationship, friendship, between God and humankind. There's a way back into the garden. Jesus has opened it up.

So it's appropriate that, when they take his dead body down from the cross and cover his nakedness with a shroud, they should place him in a garden tomb. It is in the garden that his work outside the city wall will be told and understood.

And so to this morning's story of beautiful intimacy in the garden of God's delight. Cherubim no longer on duty to keep people out of the garden, but standing at a tomb with the stone rolled back, for the one who was dead is alive again. Jesus walks in the garden, not in the cool of the evening breeze like God in Eden, but at dawn as the sun rises and begins to give its warmth. It is Mary of Magdala who sees him, standing there, seeming to be the gardener. And there is this wonderful almost wordless encounter. 'Mary!' 'Rabboni!' In that moment her fears are overcome, her grief is banished, her life is restored, her trust in God returns. Mary of Magdala is, in that moment, a kind of new Eve; Jesus, not so much the new Adam now as the glorious Son of God, the Eternal Word of the Father. For Mary, as a new Eve, as she stands there, face to face with Jesus, is a symbolic figure representing the return to relationship between God and humankind. And what that scene invites us to see is that we are invited back into the garden, back into friendship with God, back into an easy intimacy – relationship restored. 'Mary!' 'Rabboni!'

This Jesus, glorious risen Lord, still bearing the scars of his obedience, says to you today, whoever you are:

'I don't want you to be outside the beautiful place that is my kingdom, outside the garden, beyond the orbit of my love. Have you not noticed? The guards have gone. The gate is thrown open and wide. I don't see in you one weighed down by failure, disappointment, sadness, guilt. I see you, as God created you, full of potential, beautiful, with a capacity for good, for love, for flourishing. Can't you see, feel, that the failure and the sin that maybe burdened you has fallen off your back? That happened long ago when I gave *my* back to the smiters and in costly obedience to the Father's will I climbed up on that cross outside the city?

'But they buried me in a garden tomb because the garden is where I choose to be, the place of openness and joy and intimacy, where friendship can be restored, relationships deepened, life be lived with delight and expectancy.

'Will you not come back into the garden and flourish?'

Alleluia! Christ is risen!

Second Sunday of Easter, Year A

Among the stories that claim our attention in this Easter season, there is no story that I find more powerful and exciting than the one about the journey to Emmaus. It is Easter Day afternoon. Two disciples are walking from Jerusalem to the village of Emmaus. We are not even told the gender of the second one. Dispirited by the events of Good Friday, disturbed by some confusing accounts of the tomb being found empty, they are on their way to Emmaus, presumably their home. It is a story about encountering the risen Lord and there are, I want to suggest to you, four stages of that encounter, each important, each with significance for us.

The first stage is journey. Before ever we get into what was said or what happened when they reached Emmaus, just stop and think for a moment. The place they met the Lord, the place where he got in step with them, entered their conversation, was their journey. He did not join them as they stood still, but as they journeyed. It is often like that with Jesus. The risen Lord comes to those who are on the move. Of course, it is easy to come up with clichés and people often talk about life as a journey. It is bound to be that, a journey from birth to death and, in the Christian understanding, beyond that to a new life that is life indeed. In a sense, you can't help being on a journey. But there is also the opportunity to opt in to journeying, to make a decision, not to wander aimlessly, but to be on a journey, looking towards a goal, resolute about direction, disciplined about travel, wise about what you need to nourish you on your journey. For the Christian the journey is ultimately towards God and his beauty and holiness. Sometimes we describe such a journey as a pilgrimage, ourselves pilgrims travelling confidently towards the one who comes to meet us with arms outstretched in welcome.

Of course the wonder is that, though God is the ultimate goal of the journey, in Christ he is also the one who walks with us, accompanies us, encourages us. Sometimes he is at our side. Sometimes he is out ahead of us, urging us on. There are some words I love of St Bernard, writing back in the Middle Ages, that go like this:

If you stop while Jesus moves on with giant strides, not only will you fail to reach the prize, but the goal will become even more distant from you.

I love that picture of a Jesus who moves with giant strides and wants you to keep up. If we want to encounter the risen Lord, if we want to keep company with him, we need to be pilgrims, people on a very particular journey. He joins those on the move. Maybe sometimes he keeps in step. Maybe sometimes he forces the pace. He is a Jesus on the move and he is looking for people who travel, usually travel light. He is looking for pilgrims.

The second stage of encounter is the Scriptures. They are walking along, Cleopas and his companion, trying to make sense of the stupendous events of the last three days. And they are doing it through trying to interpret the Scriptures. And Jesus slides into their conversation and unfolds the meaning of the Scriptures, shows them how everything makes sense, explains how the Messiah had to suffer. He was there in their exploration of the Scriptures. And he is there for us also as we engage with the words of the Bible. He is there speaking to us, teaching us, as we work at their meaning, try to make sense of them in the context of our own day and our own lives. On the Emmaus Road they were slow to understand that it was

Jesus who had joined them. Something prevented them from recognizing him. But, as they looked back, they realized how their hearts had been burning within them as he talked to them on the road. As they looked back, they realized that they had met the Lord, encountered Christ, in their engagement with the Scriptures. It hadn't been straightforward and easy. It hardly ever is with the Bible. Hardly ever is it easy faith or easy rules for Christian living, handed to you on a plate. Nearly always it is hard graft, a bit of a struggle. But it's worth working away at it, knowing that he, our risen Lord, can be met in his word and that it can be a life-shaping, life-changing encounter.

We encounter Christ in the journey. We encounter Christ in the Scriptures. The third stage is that we encounter him in the meal, the meal the Church calls by a lot of names – the sacrament, the Lord's Supper, Holy Communion, the Eucharist, the Breaking of Bread, the Mass. With all its infinite and rich variety, it is, in this story, a profound setting for encountering the risen Lord. They have arrived in their village. Jesus makes as if to go on. But they persuade him to stay with them. They sit down to supper, bread on the table, may be wine also, and this is when he does his characteristic thing, the thing the Gospels tell us he often did – feeding a crowd of 5,000, feeding another multitude of 4,000, taking bread into his hands at the supper the night before he died. It was when he did that, the way he did it, that was the moment when their eyes were opened and they knew – 'it is the Lord!' A wonderful moment of revelation. It was in the meal that they recognized him.

And, again, it should be the same for us. Jesus urged his followers to take bread and wine, to give thanks, to break the bread, to share, to do what he had done with them so often, and most significantly, on that night before he died, and now, just as significantly, on this night of his resurrection, and so to remember him. And the word he used for 'remember' is a very strong word. It means much more than strain the memory to recall something in the past. It is not about straining the memory for something half forgotten that might otherwise be completely lost. It is about re-living with such intensity that past and present merge. For the Israelite people this is exactly what happened each year in the Passover festival. They re-lived the exodus from Egypt with such imagination that the past was drawn wonderfully into the present, so that it was not so much that they recalled how the Lord had saved their ancestors at the Red Sea, but that, powerfully present in their midst, the Lord was saving them now.

It is something of that that is going on in the meal Christians share in remembrance of Christ. The Church remembers the meal in the upper room or the supper table at Emmaus with such prayerful imagination and intensity that the *presence* of the Lord – not the memory, but the presence – is experienced in the unfolding of the Scriptures and in the breaking of the bread. The past is drawn into the present and Jesus stands there in our midst, host more than guest, in response to our remembering. He is with us as we take the bread and the wine, as we give thanks, as we break, as we share. We encounter not a dead hero, in the end not just, not only, the victim of Calvary, but a risen, a living Lord.

We encounter Christ in the journey. We encounter Christ in the Scriptures. We encounter Christ in the meal.

Fourth, finally, look more precisely at what they identified as the moment of recognition. As I said, the Church has lots of names for the sacred meal. They are all good words. But did you see what they called it in this story? They called it the 'Breaking of the Bread'. 'They told what had happened on the road, and how he had been made known to them in the breaking of the bread.'

There's a moment in the meal when the bread is broken. At one level it is a very practical thing. You can't share a loaf unless you break it up. But actually there's something much more symbolic, much more profound, going on when we break the bread. The body of the Lord was broken upon the cross for the redemption of the world. It was only the broken body that could redeem. When we come to communion what needs to be placed in our hands shouldn't be something round, smooth, aesthetic, but something ragged, jagged, clearly broken off from something else. And that's partly a reminder that what Christ gives us we share with others – it's never a private personal thing. But, more deeply, it is a sign that Christ is often encountered in brokenness. We look upon his brokenness – for even our risen Lord still bears the scars – and he looks upon our brokenness. We are, for the most part, ragged, jagged, aching souls. He looks upon our brokenness and he offers us the healing that comes from the cross. We encounter this wounded Lord in our brokenness, in the brokenness of our world, and we find life and healing.

We encounter Christ in the journey. We encounter Christ in the Scriptures. We encounter Christ in the meal. We encounter. Christ in the brokenness. It's wonderful good news, real gospel, isn't it, that we can meet him in these ways?

Baptism and Confirmation

It's great that no less than nine of us take an important step today. Thank you to them for doing so. Thank you also to all who have brought them to this moment. A great day!

All the better because it is Easter. To be more precise, the 15th day of Easter and Easter has another 35 days to run, through Ascension Day and on to Pentecost. So all thoughts of Easter eggs may have gone and Easter holidays over, but still we celebrate the Church's Easter faith and the heart of what Christians believe – that Jesus died on the cross for the sins of the world and God raised him gloriously to life again on Easter Day. Yes, Alleluia, Christ is risen.

So all the better because it is Easter and today we celebrate three Easter sacraments.

The first is baptism. Two of the candidates are to be baptized. The other candidates, gathering around the font with them, will be sprinkled with the water from the font to remind them of their baptism, however many years ago that was. Indeed, all of us will be put in mind of our own baptism into Christ. It is an Easter sacrament because what it celebrates is our acceptance of Jesus' way, which is to die to the old and to rise to the new, to bury the old and to burst, as if out of the grave, into the life of the new, as Jesus did on the first Easter Day.

Yes, Easter calls us to walk with the risen Lord, trying to conform ourselves to his wonderful pattern of dying and living, witnessing like him to the truth that the love of God is stronger than death. Baptism – an Easter sacrament.

Second, confirmation. The candidates renew their relationship with God as they confirm their faith and, even more importantly, God confirms his love for them and the gift of his Holy Spirit to strengthen them and give them life. It's an Easter sacrament, for it is the same Holy Spirit that we celebrate in them that Jesus breathed on his disciples on Easter Day, when he appeared to them in the upper room and said, 'Peace be with you. Receive the Holy Spirit.' It's an Easter sacrament, for the same Holy Spirit we celebrate in them is the Holy Spirit who, when the 50 days of Easter were complete, was poured upon the Church on the day of Pentecost, giving them the confidence to speak of their faith and draw others to Christ.

And then we gather around the Lord's table for the Eucharist, the first time that most of the nine here will have received Holy Communion. You may not think that Holy Communion is quite so special; after all, it's something we celebrate week in week out. But, do you know, it should always be special for each one of us, first communion or 500th communion, whenever we come, however often we come, for it is, every time, a meeting point with Jesus and spiritual food for the journey of life, just as it was for those disciples of whom St Luke speaks who, at the end of their journey to Emmaus on Easter evening, inviting Jesus to have supper with them, recognized the risen Lord when he took the bread and gave thanks to God, then broke it. What they shared, what we share, every time we come is the life of the risen Lord. Never take the Eucharist for granted. We meet Jesus in the breaking of the bread; it is a quite wonderful gift.

Baptism, confirmation, Holy Communion – three Easter sacraments, each one a huge blessing. Praise the Lord!

Three Easter sacraments. And there are three truths I want you to hang on to from this evening. They are centred on these three words – individuality, company and vocation.

Individuality. For all that we are a bit of a crowd tonight, there are some moments for each of you being baptized and confirmed that are very individual, personal. At those moments you stand apart from everyone else. I shall ask individually: 'Is this your faith?' and they say 'This is my faith.' Not our faith, not the faith *of the Church* – though both are true – but my faith. It is a moment of personal testimony.

A little later each candidate says to me 'I am Emily', 'I am Wally', 'I am Innez' or whatever their name. For what God is about to confirm is who each one of them is, who they are, with all their individualism, each unique personality whom he loves. And, in response, before I anoint them with the holy oil and place my hand on their head, I look them in the eye and say their name, adding 'God has called you by name and made you his own.' God calls you by your name, just as, in the garden on Easter Day, he called Mary Magdalene by her name, 'Mary!' That was the moment when her fears and sorrows fell away and she knew his love and his faithfulness. God calls you by name and makes you his own. It's a deeply personal individual moment, for God does not love us simply as part of a crowd, but for who we uniquely are. And there are moments all through our Christian lives when we need to be able to stand alone, to be ourselves, but always to know ourselves affirmed and loved.

But the second word is 'company'. God has made us to belong, made us for friendship, made us for fellowship. Even when we stand alone, hovering around us are those whom he has given us to be our companions. God who is himself Trinity wants us also always to be in company. And so this afternoon, for instance, when I ask whether this is their faith, it is faith that the entire congregation has just spelt out in solidarity with all the candidates. And when we come to the confirmation, the candidates will all sense the support of family, godparents and of the whole Church, providing encouragement and companionship in faith. And when you receive the body and blood of Christ in the Eucharist, for all that it will be a deeply personal moment, it will also be in company, people sharing with you the meal that Christians share. The company that you join in your baptism, that supports you at your confirmation, shares with you in the Eucharist, is the one holy catholic and apostolic Church, the Church of all times and all places. Faith and discipleship are deeply personal things, but God's will for us is to experience them in company, in the company of today's disciples of Jesus Christ, the fellowship of the baptized. Stick with the Church, love her like Jesus loves her. Even when she drives you to distraction, don't give up on her. She won't give up on you. If you wander off, you can always come back and find a welcome.

And to my final truth. Part of what God wants each one of us to discover is our own unique vocation, what he wants each one of us to do with our lives. Confirmation can be a moment when that becomes clear. Attending somebody else's confirmation can be a moment when that becomes clear. Or maybe a confirmation is just a moment when a seed is planted and we hardly notice at the time. I'd love to come back next year because people today decide that it is time for them to take the next step and to be confirmed and to become one of those who shares the Eucharist around the altar table. Think about it. Maybe God is prompting you now.

But vocation is about much more than that. It is about what God wants us to do with our lives. These people being confirmed need to listen to see what God is saying to them about what he wants them to do with the rest of their lives. I can't know what that is. But God knows and wants you to find out. There are many different kinds of vocation.

Not all of them look the slightest bit churchy. But some do and probably here in the church somewhere tonight is someone whom God is calling to a very specific ministry in the Church. Hidden in among you is probably a man or a woman, a boy or a girl, whom God wants to be a priest. It's one of the great questions of our life and it keeps coming back: 'What does God want me to do now?'

Individuality, company, vocation. God confirms the unique you, God gives you the people of God to be your companions on the way, God calls you on and invites you to discover with him what he wants you to do with the rest of your life. God confirms that and much more than that today as we celebrate baptism, confirmation and the Eucharist, three Easter sacraments of the risen Lord.

Fifth Sunday of Easter, Year C

The Fifth Sunday of Easter – 29 days into a 50-day season. Your first joy in the resurrection has probably been replaced by a gentler more reflective celebration of that stupendous truth that by the power of his love God raised Jesus. But Easter has to be our starting point. We're given this lovely season of seven weeks of seven days from Easter Day to Pentecost to explore the implications for ourselves, for the Church and for the world of that act of God whereby the risen Lord burst from the tomb, wonderfully, gloriously alive. To explore and, of course, to celebrate.

And that, of course, is why in Eastertide we read the Acts of the Apostles, for, though it begins with the ascension of Jesus and ends with Paul a prisoner in Rome, it is really about how the Church, animated by the Holy Spirit, spread the Easter faith. The Acts of the Apostles is the working through of the resurrection.

And today we hear about the widening of the orbit of the resurrection faith. Easter begins with that little committed band that had become disciples. In the garden on Easter morning, on the walk to Emmaus, over breakfast at the lakeside, in the upper room behind locked doors, committed followers discovered the aliveness of Jesus Christ, encountered the risen Lord. It seemed at first as if it was for them.

But Paul tells us that there was one appearance to more than 500 people at once. And then there was Pentecost and Peter preaching about the resurrection to all those people we read about in Acts chapter 2 who had come from all over the world to Jerusalem. It sounds very international, the list of places from which they came. But they were all of the Jewish faith, come to the holy city for the feast. But the orbit has widened. The Easter faith is not for the few, but for the many, for the whole Jewish people.

And then comes our story today from Acts 11. It's told twice, once when it happens, once when Peter needs to give an account of it to people who were suspicious. Why has he been eating with Gentiles? Why has he been sharing the good news with Gentiles? Why has he been baptizing Gentiles? And he tells the story of his vision, of the clear message from God, on which he acts. The good news is for the Gentiles too. And to confirm it the Holy Spirit comes upon them also. The orbit of the resurrection is the whole world.

The Holy Spirit – here is another wonderful experience of expansion. The influence of the Spirit, like the orbit of resurrection, is greater than they had at first thought. After all, on Easter evening, it was only on that little group hiding in the upper room behind locked doors that Jesus had breathed the Spirit – 'Peace be with you. Receive the Holy Spirit.' The Spirit was just for them. But then comes Pentecost and the Spirit comes in a much more dramatic way; a lot of them are out on the streets empowered by the Spirit, and it all seems to be spreading and the Spirit is being given all over the place. It's very exciting, but it is only for the Jewish people. But then comes our story. Listen to what Peter said:

And as I began to speak, the Holy Spirit fell upon them just as it had upon us at the beginning. And I remembered the word of the Lord, how he had said, 'John baptized with water, but you will be baptized with the Holy Spirit.' If then God gave them the same gift that he gave us when we believed in the Lord Jesus Christ, who was I that I could hinder God? (Acts 11.15–17)

The orbit of the resurrection is the whole world. The influence of the Spirit is universal.

And so what is emerging there is a Christianity that is an inclusive faith. Not a universal faith in the sense of one that says that everybody will be saved, but an inclusive one that says that anybody can be if they are open to the Spirit and honour the name of Christ. Of course, the implication was always there, though it took the Church a time to understand what God was saying. After all, as John tells it, Jesus understood his death on the cross as having a meaning for the whole world. 'I, if I am lifted up from the earth, will draw everyone to myself.' Not just the little band of followers, not just one chosen race, the whole world drawn to himself. And we echo that every week in the Eucharist. 'Lamb of God, you take away the sin of the world.' It's wonderfully inclusive. It reflects, of course, an all-embracing generous God, the one who longs that all his sons and daughters will recognize him and come back to him.

An all-embracing generous inclusive God implies something inescapably important for the Church. It implies a Church with open doors, probably with ragged edges, with a welcoming stance, a non-judgemental, generous, inclusive Church. There have been times when the Church has really not looked as if that is what it wants to be. In our own day, I do believe that we want to be all those things, and indeed are desperate to be seen and believed to be all those things. We want to be generous, we want to be welcoming, we want to be inclusive. Praise the Lord for that. But, of course, it is not as easy as it looks. Quite apart from the failures in our local churches sometimes to be all those things, there are the tensions you cannot avoid in the Anglican Communion, about such issues as the ordination of women as priests and bishops and about the place of gay people in the Church's life and leadership. It all sounds easy, at first. If there is an inclusive God, then the Church's ministry ought to be inclusive, so why should women not be priests and bishops? If there is an inclusive God, then the Church's membership ought to be inclusive, so why should gay people not have an equal place?

But, of course, it isn't that easy, for the Holy Spirit is a Spirit to lead us into all truth and there are those – and they have some unavoidable passages of Scripture on their side – whose understanding of truth leads them to set limits, to guard tradition, to take a stand for biblical truths as they understand them. And those are honest positions that we have to honour and take seriously. We need to be a listening Church. We need to be a patient Church. We need to recognize that some talk of 'inclusive Church' doesn't take seriously enough the call to faith and to repentance that was part of the message that Peter preached in the house at Joppa. 'God has given to the Gentiles the repentance that leads to life' is not a promise of unconditional belonging. Faith and repentance are required of us all and seeing where that is needed is not always as straightforward as it sounds. Nevertheless, we do well, as we struggle with these things, in our own hearts and in the debates within the Church, to remember that we are trying to discern the will of a generous, welcoming, inclusive God. That's our starting point.

Let's turn to the Gospel reading. It's from John chapter 13 and that context is significant, for John 13 is the chapter where, on the night before his passion, Jesus washes the feet of his disciples. We are reading it, of course, not in Passiontide, but in Eastertide, and I guess we are given it today because the words of Jesus, 'I am with you only a little longer, where I am going you cannot come', begin to tune us into the next phase of the Easter season, when the Lord returns to the Father at the ascension. But the washing of the feet of the disciples on Maundy Thursday night was an act of humility and service and, above all else, love. Having done it, he tells them to wash one another's feet. And in the passage we heard today, as Jesus talks to his friends, he spells that out, 'I give you a new commandment, that you love one another.' Not only must they wash one another's feet; they must love one another. Indeed, if they wash one another's feet, it is because they love one another.

His motive on that dark Thursday evening was love. It was love because, everywhere he went and in everything he did, Jesus echoed, modelled, exemplified the love of the one who sent him, the one who so loved the world that he gave his only Son. We are to love one another because Christ loved, loves, us, because the Easter God is love.

That links with our earlier theme inspired by Peter and the Acts of the Apostles. God is a welcoming, generous, inclusive God, because love is his nature, love is his character, love is his name. How could God be anything but welcoming, generous, inclusive when God is love? It brings us back to where we began. How is it that Jesus was raised? He was raised by the power of God's love. Death could not hold him, for love, God's love, is stronger than death.

Rejoice in this Easter season.

Rejoice that the orbit of the resurrection is the whole world.

Rejoice that the influence of the Holy Spirit is universal.

Rejoice in a generous welcoming inclusive Easter God.

Rejoice in the power of his love.

Ascension Day

Put alongside the account of the ascension we heard from Acts, if you will, this picture:

> But while he was still far off, his father saw him and was filled with compassion; he ran and put his arms around him and kissed him ... the father said to his slaves, 'Quickly, bring out a robe – the best one – and put it on him; put a ring on his finger and sandals on his feet. And get the fatted calf and kill it, and let us eat and celebrate; for this son of mine was dead and is alive again; he was lost and is found!' (Luke 15.20–24)

Forget the fatted calf, which one imagines has no place in heaven, and isn't that a quite wonderful picture of the other side of the cloud, so to speak? Earthbound disciples staring into the sky could not see it, but in the imagination we can see the Father, enveloping the Son in his embrace, the Son who has come home.

And yet you will not have failed to recognize the description, one from the lips of Jesus himself, as he tells in Luke chapter 15 his story of the prodigal son. At a certain level, therefore, it is an inappropriate text to use of the least of prodigal sons – extravagant, yes, extravagant in his loving, but not prodigal. In Luke's story the son goes to a distant country, armed with his share of the father's wealth and squanders it in dissolute living. But Jesus is the Son sent by the Father to a distant land, laying aside his riches, becoming poor for our sake, and going about, doing good and healing all manner of diseases among the people. So, yes, this Son of the Father is a very different one – and yet, the kiss, the robe, the ring, and then those powerful words 'this son of mine was dead and is alive again; he was lost and is found'. This is the Son who ascended the cross and died there for the redemption of all who have sinned against heaven. This is the Son who lost his life. This is the Son who descended to the dead. This is the Son who nevertheless is alive again. He it is around whom the Father puts his arms, welcomes him home and kisses him.

There is a beautiful poem by the Welsh poet Saunders Lewis entitled 'Ascension Thursday', in which the elevation of the host at the Eucharist is likened to the Ascension and images of the Father warmly embracing the Son.

'The Father kissing the Son in the white dew.' Ascension is, essentially, the feast of the return to the Father. Not just, as we have heard it thus today from Luke in the Acts of the Apostles, but as John describes different chronology, where, on Easter Day, Jesus says to Mary Magdalene, 'Go and tell my brothers that I am ascending to my Father and your Father, to my God and your God.' It is the reuniting of Father and Son, as Jesus returns to him mission accomplished, his obedience to the Father's will complete.

The Scriptures do not give many stories of 'return to the Father'. Moses disappears on the mountain. Elijah goes up in a whirlwind. Enoch ascends. The Christian tradition pictures Mary arriving in the heavenly realm to be crowned by her Saviour Son. But there is no return quite like the return of the only begotten Son to the Father. The picture of the embrace, the kiss, of welcome home is a powerful one and the story we so often describe as the parable of the prodigal son is, in fact, much more the story of the compassionate loving Father. It was that compassionate loving that motivated the eternal Father to send the only-begotten Son into the world. 'God so loved the world.' It was to tell of that compassionate loving Father that Jesus told his parable. It was that compassionate loving that allowed the Son to be sacrificed on the altar of the cross. It was that compassionate loving that rolled back the stone, loving the Son back to life. 'He was dead and is alive again, was lost and is found.' It was all by the Father's compassionate loving.

Jesus is always seen as the pioneer, the one who blazes the trail. In his resurrection he is the firstfruits of the harvest of the dead. In his ascension he goes before us, showing us the way. We are all to be drawn to the Father, all to see him coming towards us with arms of welcome, all to receive his kiss of peace, all to have a festal robe placed on us. Our approach will be more like that of the *prodigal* son. 'Father, I have sinned against heaven and before you and am no longer worthy to be called your child.' But such is the nature of God, that, whether we come like Jesus, sinless, innocent and obedient, or whether we come like the prodigal – broken, guilty and penitent – the welcome is the same. Love knows no reception but welcome and embrace.

And the journey has, of course, begun. In a sense, the growing conformity of Jesus to the Father's will through baptism, transfiguration, agony and crucifixion was always a journey back to the Father. Perhaps only when the sky turned black that Friday afternoon did he fail to see the Father moving towards him, his arms outstretched in welcome. For us also the sense of being drawn back to the Father has begun. The scholars puzzle over the present tense of 'I am ascending to my Father' in John chapter 20. But ascension as a process, as a journey, is true to our experiences too. The cords of love draw us slowly yet surely. The arms beckon from afar. But we know the home towards which we are being drawn and we experience already the love that will enfold us.

If 'Christ is risen' is the oft-repeated message of the Easter season, 'Christ is risen' with its cascades of alleluias, the ascension introduces another catchphrase, just as scriptural, a key affirmation for the earliest Christians. 'Jesus is Lord.' Each year it adds something crucial as we move towards Pentecost.

'Jesus is Lord.' It matters how you say it. With the emphasis on the third word, which is how you most often hear it, 'Jesus is *Lord*', the intention is to tell us something about Jesus. Lordship is assumed. Power, sovereignty, dominion, authority and the whole concept that we associate with lordship, is given to Jesus, because he has achieved a victory, triumphed, defeated the enemy. We are still in the language of power. 'Jesus is Lord' is a Jesus in majesty. And that has its place and Scripture affirms it.

But say it in a different way. It's the way Bishop John V. Taylor always urged it to be said. '*Jesus* is Lord.' Do you hear the difference? No longer is Jesus being defined in terms of lordship. Instead, lordship is being redefined in terms of what we know of Jesus. And the Jesus we have learned about, the Jesus who has accomplished the Father's will and is now returning to his home, is the self-emptying servant of simplicity, humility, vulnerability and suffering. That is the Jesus we have encountered, expressing the Father's will, and he is Lord – and, in so being, redefines lordship. It isn't the way we thought it was. It isn't the way the world thinks it is. It is one of the divine contradictions that, if *Jesus* is Lord, lordship is servanthood, power is weakness, wealth is poverty. Oh yes, it is all turned upside down by the one who now returns to the Father.

And in the Father kissing the Son, we see the truth that Jesus had shared, 'I and the Father are one.' In that coming together, that embrace, we can see that it is not that Jesus brings something new into the godhead from his adventures on earth, as if humanity was now drawn into divinity to supply a lack, but that for the first time we can see that simplicity, humility, vulnerability, suffering have always been part of the character of the servant God, the loving Father. The Son and the Father are one. What the Son revealed on earth, living in conformity to the Father's will, is the eternal nature of the Father. And that, above all else, is what is revealed to us when the Father goes out to meet the Son, to embrace him and welcome him home:

His father saw him and was filled with compassion; he ran and put his arms around him and kissed him ... the father said to his slaves, 'Quickly, bring out a robe – the best one ... put a ring on his finger and sandals on his feet ... and let us eat and celebrate; for this son of mine was dead and is alive again; he was lost and is found!' (Luke 15.20–24)

... come ... to see
The elevation of the unblemished host
And the Father kissing the Son in the white dew.
(Saunders Lewis)

The Feast of Pentecost

Seven weeks of seven days have passed since we had on our lips the Easter greeting 'Christ is risen' and here this afternoon we have greeted one another with it again for the last time this year as we focus on the last of the great truths that Easter proclaims. The truth is this: the Lord is with us till the end of time because the Holy Spirit is always being poured upon us. The Holy Spirit is being poured out just as John describes it in the upper room on the evening of the resurrection, the first day of Easter, and just as Luke describes it in the same upper room, as we have heard this afternoon, on this, the fiftieth day.

But let us be clear. Pentecost does not mark the first coming into the world of God's Spirit, as if there had been no Holy Spirit before. The Scriptures tell us that the Spirit of God brooded over the waters at the creation. In other words, the Holy Spirit has always and everywhere been the agent of God's activity – not only in the Church, not only in the Christian era, but always and everywhere.

And if we move into New Testament times, it is the Holy Spirit who activates the body of Mary to develop within it the life that would be Christ. Remember the words of the angel:

The Holy Spirit will come upon you, and the power of the Most High will overshadow you. (Luke 1.35)

And in the Creed we proclaim that Jesus Christ

was incarnate from the Holy Spirit and the Virgin Mary.

This all long before Pentecost. And then remember Jesus at the beginning of his ministry, preaching in the synagogue in Capernaum, and declaring, with echoes of Isaiah:

The Spirit of the Lord is upon me, because he has anointed me ... (Luke 4.18)

And that he knew this to be the case, not just from inner conviction, but from that dramatic descent of the Holy Spirit like a dove that had marked his baptism in the Jordan river.

The Holy Spirit of God is much more than a kind of shadow of the Jesus who walked upon this earth. The Spirit is much more than a continuance of the life of Jesus. The Spirit is the living God operating at key moments in the life of humanity and in every individual human life. At the creation, at the conception of Christ, at his baptism, there is God engaging with his handiwork through the activity of the Holy Spirit.

So what is so special about Pentecost? Why hail it as the climax of the Easter faith and the beginning of a whole new phase in the world's salvation? There is more than one answer to that, but here is one answer about which to think this afternoon. It is because Pentecost is like a new creation, a new conception. Let me try to show you what that means.

At the creation, the Holy Spirit was at work, not only in the brooding over the waters that Genesis describes, but in the creation of humankind:

The LORD God formed man from the dust of the ground, and breathed into his nostrils the breath of life; and the man became a living being. (Gen. 2.7)

That's the Spirit, the breath, the life God implanted, giving Adam a share in the divine life. Adam was to live on earth the life that God lived in heaven. And Adam was to care for the world, the creation entrusted to him, on God's behalf. The Spirit breathed into Adam in order that Adam might reflect

God's life and care for the world: that was the way it was supposed to be. And however much we regard Adam not as an individual historical man, but as a sort of representative figure for humankind, it remains true that God's intention was that humankind should reflect God's nature and share his work. That was why his Spirit was implanted within it.

But it went wrong. The Scriptures are clear about that. Humankind went its own way, tarnished God's image, misused the creation entrusted to it, lost sight of innocence, and would not listen to the voice in the wind, the voice of the Spirit. The disorder, the chaos, that ensued in God's world is typified by that strange tale in Genesis chapter 11 of the Tower of Babel, where such is the confusion that people cease to understand one another and talk in a variety of untranslatable tongues. God's great enterprise was in trouble.

There is, of course, a kind of ambivalence in Scripture about the fall. No part of the creation is exempt from it. Its consequences are found in every aspect of our lives. And yet, because of the faithfulness of God, the story – even without Jesus – is not one of unmitigated disaster. Sin takes hold, the image of the divine is tarnished, yet communion with the Creator is still possible; creativity – human and divine – continues, and goodness, beauty, love and compassion can still motivate.

And the reason for that is that the Holy Spirit is never withdrawn. Despite the fall, the breath breathed into Adam still animates the human soul. And that is an important truth. The Spirit was not withdrawn from the human race, locked away again in the life of the Trinity until released into the body of Mary, or of Jesus, or of the Church at Pentecost. The Spirit would not be contained. The Spirit unfailingly through human history inspired and enlivened and drew out of men and women all that is good and honest and true. 'The Spirit of the Lord fills the universe.' That is not a Pentecost message. It is a creation message. And it is a message that guards against making today's celebration too narrowly churchy. The Spirit now, as always, animates the world.

Yet, because there is a fatal flaw that the Scriptures describe in terms of the fall of Adam, there is another truth to set alongside that truth of the Spirit's continuity. It is the truth that in Jesus God would begin again, a new conception, a new Adam. In Jesus the Spirit of God would not be squeezed out by selfishness and sin; the image would not be tarnished. He would be a faithful steward of the creation. He would care for the world.

So once again you see 'Operation Holy Spirit', as the Prayer Book all but calls it. The Spirit comes into the body of Mary and she conceives her Son. And later the Holy Spirit descends upon the Lord and he knows himself called to this vocation to restore what had been lost in Adam. In Christ the Holy Spirit dwelt, giving him power, enabling people to see in him the clue to the nature of God.

But, if Christ is to return to the Father, how is this new sort of humanity, this new humankind, restored to God's image, this new caring for the world, to be perpetuated? Once again the answer lay in the infusion of the Holy Spirit into a body, so that the body might radiate God's life. The Holy Spirit had made fertile the womb of Mary in order that Jesus Christ might live among us for a season and teach us the path of life. And now at Pentecost the Holy Spirit made fertile the body of Christ – not the body that had been buried in the tomb, but the mystical body, the spiritual body, the group of followers who were now to be Christ in the world. John has Jesus breathing life into his disciples on Easter Day, just as God had breathed life into Adam on creation day; and as he does so he says 'Receive the Holy Spirit'. It is a new creation, a new conception.

And so, alongside the truth of a Spirit who fills the world, who animates all living things and inspires the human race, we are given another truth of a Spirit who has a special sphere of operation in the Church. The task of the Church, this new body of Christ, is to continue the work of Jesus, to make secure for all time his reversal of the Old Testament calamity, where God's enterprise went wrong to the extent that people were so divided that they failed to understand what one another were saying. No wonder the miracle of Pentecost is portrayed in terms of everybody suddenly understanding one another's language – all those Parthians, Medes and Elamites, and others too, drawn together back into a common humanity. That is the task of the Church, to secure for all time, by the preaching of the gospel and the bringing of people to Christ, the reversal of the Old Testament calamity. It is a task that involves holding fast to the image of God, preserving it as untarnished as human beings can, keeping the sense of life lived in the Spirit alive for humankind, living on earth the way God lives in heaven.

And so, of course, as the Holy Spirit was breathed into the body of Adam so that he might come alive, for a task in which he failed, and as the Holy Spirit was breathed into the body of Mary so that Jesus might come to life, for the task in which he was gloriously faithful, so the Holy Spirit is breathed into the body of the Church so that it, that we, may come alive, for the task that is laid upon us.

Today's festival provides a marvellous opportunity to reclaim the great stories of the giving of the Spirit at key moments in the tale of salvation and, in the re-living of them, to say with special longing at Pentecost each year, 'Come, Holy Spirit, fill the hearts of your faithful people.' Nevertheless, these are simply moments that we claim to celebrate eternal timeless truths. Just as the Holy Spirit ever hovers over the creation, else it would cease to be, and breathes life into every person, lest they also cease to be, so the Holy Spirit indwells the Church every moment of every day, animates and encourages without ceasing, lest it fade away and fail, a sacred mystery gone to rack and ruin. We celebrate that truth of the Spirit's indwelling every week in the Eucharist, asking for the gift of the Holy Spirit to come upon the bread and wine and upon the people. Every day the Spirit is renewed among us.

Creation, Christ, Church. Into all three the Holy Spirit of God comes so that God's life may be available to all, God's power may be known in his creation, and God's love may fill our hearts.

Come, Holy Spirit.
Renew the creation.
Show us the Father.
Keep us faithful to Christ.
Fill our hearts.

Trinity Sunday

This is a wonderful day. It's a wonderful day because it is the Feast of the Holy Trinity and that makes it for the whole Church a principal holy day. It puts it on a par with Christmas, Easter, Ascension, Pentecost. That's the theory; the reality is that it is not a source of excitement in many places I know. But I need to tell you that for me it really is a wonderful day and celebrates something overwhelmingly important, immensely joy-making and extraordinarily challenging. All those things because it celebrates God and draws us into the mystery of his being and his loving and invites us to join in.

The extraordinary thing is that people have made the Trinity difficult. No, that's a silly thing to say; there *are* issues – theological issues – that the scholars engage with in trying to give some definition to the nature of God. The Athanasian Creed is evidence of that and we shouldn't be slipshod in our theological reflection. But there are simple and lovely things to say about the Trinity and these are what people need to hear.

There are five simple and lovely truths I want to share with you briefly today.

The first is this. The Trinity is a mystery. But it is not the kind of mystery you need to solve. It is not the kind of mystery you have to explain. It is a mystery you are invited to enter and to enjoy. If you've never done it (though you probably have without knowing it), then when you do you will find it is like entering a new relationship. There's joy, there's surprise, there's a bit of puzzlement ('What's happening to me here?' you say), there's a sense of being drawn deeper, there is energy, there is love. And, if you *have* done it, and you know that entering the mystery of the Trinity is like that – is like committing yourself to a friend or a lover – then you also know that if you neglect that relationship, or take it for granted but come back to it with your eyes open wider, there's new potential for joy, for surprise, for puzzlement ('What's happening to me now?' you say) and, yes, wonderfully, drawn deeper still. That's the way it can be for you and me with God, who is Trinity. The Trinity is a mystery into which we can enter.

The second thing is this. What we find at the heart of the mystery – no, that's wrong; we've not yet, any of us I think, penetrated to the heart of the mystery – no, as soon as we allow ourselves to be drawn in at all, is overwhelming love. But it is not all that we meet. We see unutterable beauty. We encounter unimaginable holiness. We witness unexpected intimacy. We are touched by transforming grace. But what we meet first and experience most deeply, if only we can open ourselves, body, mind and spirit, our entire being with its longings, is love.

For what the Trinity is about is the Father loving the Son; the Son loving the Father; the Spirit the love that flows between them. It is the life, the love, that was there before the world was made. It is the life, the love, that was there before Jesus walked the earth; the Father loving the Son, the Son loving the Father; the Spirit the love that flows between them.

W. H. Vanstone expressed this in *Love's Endeavour, Love's Expense*. He wrote:

In the dynamic relationship within the being of the Trinity, love is already present, already active, already completed and already triumphant: for the love of the Father meets with the perfect response of the Son. Each, one might say, endlessly enriches the other: and this rich and dynamic interrelationship is the being and life of the Spirit.

It is, of course, the love that caused the Father to send the Son. It is the love that came down at Christmas. It is the love that took Jesus to the cross. It is the love that burst the tomb open. It is the love that was poured out on Mary at the annunciation, on Jesus at his baptism, on the Church on the day of Pentecost. It is the love that enfolds us from birth to death and beyond. But it has its existence, has its reality, in the being of the Trinity.

The Trinity is a mystery into which we can enter. When we enter it we are enfolded by love.

The third thing is this. This creative love is never used up, never drained dry, is always recreating, always refreshing, and – this is the crucial truth – always overflowing. Within the Trinity there is more love than is needed, more love than can be contained. It overflows and it runs all over the earth and it enters every human heart that is ready to receive it, taking away the heart of stone. Flowing from the godhead, flowing from the loving of the Father and the Son and the Holy Spirit, is enough love, and more than enough, to sustain the world God first created out of love and then redeemed by love.

The Trinity is a mystery into which we can enter. When we enter it we are enfolded by love. The love from the Trinity overflows over the earth.

The fourth thing is this. We do not have to draw very near to this mystery of the Trinity before we find ourselves being beckoned into its life, its love. We have, perhaps, over-used that wonderful icon by Rublev called 'the hospitality of Abraham'. But we have used it because it expresses the invitation of the Trinity so beautifully and visually. The three visitors to Abraham, who one moment seem to be men and the next angels, and the next the three persons of the godhead, sit around the table, on which food is placed, and seem to draw you in to occupy a fourth place, to share their food, their intimacy, their love, their life. In prayer you are being drawn into the divine loving, even when you cannot sense it. In the Eucharist you are being drawn into the divine loving, even when you forget it. Here today something of that is going on. Entering the mystery is exactly what God wants us to do. We do not need to hold back or to be afraid, for we do not need to be worthy to enter. We need to be a little bit vulnerable, but then who of us isn't? He draws us in with cords of love.

The Trinity is a mystery into which we can enter. When we enter it we are enfolded by love. The love from the Trinity overflows over the earth. It is God's deep desire that we shall indeed enter in and share the life of the Trinity.

The fifth, the final, thing is this. The love that draws us in, and never entirely lets us go, nevertheless sends us out, renewed and refreshed by our experience of the beauty, the holiness, the intimacy and the grace, filled with the love, to go with the flow of the love that runs over the earth. We need always to know ourselves to be deeply loved, even when we mess up, receive extra love when we mess up and therefore need the love the more, and to know ourselves to be channels of love, helping the love that flows from the Trinity to reach those margins of the world where people can hardly believe it is love for them. To each one of us God, who is Trinity, says, know yourself always deeply loved and, whenever we are strong enough to hear it, God adds, 'Go with the flow of that love, helping it to reach those margins of the world where people can hardly believe it is love for them.'

The Trinity is a mystery into which we can enter. When we enter it we are enfolded by love. The love from the Trinity overflows over the earth. It is God's deep desire that we shall indeed enter in and share the life of the Trinity. It is our mission to go with the flow of love and help it to reach the unexpecting places where people cry out for love.

And may the Father, the Son and the Holy Spirit, Holy and undivided Trinity, Three Persons in one God, enfolding you always in his love, make you effective in your mission.

Corpus Christi

I am a bit suspicious of preachers who very often talk about themselves. 'We preach *Christ Jesus* and ourselves as your servants for Jesus' sake,' as the apostle Paul puts it. But today I will speak personally. And what I want to say is very simple but to me very important.

Essentially it is this. Of all the invitations Jesus issues in the gospel story, one that we hear less about has turned out for me to be crucially important. It isn't 'Follow me' – we all know that invitation. And, yes, I have tried to follow him, and so have you. 'Take up your cross' – there's another invitation. Harder, more immediate, and obviously challenging. But we Christians are marked with the cross. And, yes, I have tried to take up my cross, and if I am asked one day to take up a heavier cross I hope I will be given the grace to carry that too. And there are people here no doubt who have walked patiently with heavy crosses to bear and have been given the grace to do it well.

But the invitation I want to talk about is this: 'Come and eat.' It is found only in one story, an Easter story, when Jesus stands on the lakeside and calls to the fishermen-disciples to come and have breakfast. And yet of course in another sense he's always saying 'Come and eat', whether it be to a crowd of 5,000, or to tax-gatherers and sinners, or to the Twelve on the night before he died, or the two friends after the walk to Emmaus. It's always 'Come and eat' and it is always bread that is on the menu.

In my Christian pilgrimage, I have heard that invitation of Jesus more clearly than any other. Even when I haven't quite been able to make out what following him might mean, even when I am rather resistant to taking up the cross, or simply can't fathom what is being asked of me, I've understood 'Come and eat' and I've done it. I've knelt, I guess, at a thousand different altars, and at least half heard the unchanging words – 'This is my body, this is my blood, do this in remembrance of me' – and stretched out hands and taken what was offered, and eaten. And even when I'm not feeling very religious, or very prayerful, even when it's difficult to concentrate on the words of the service because something else is filling my mind, I keep hearing that invitation 'Come and eat'.

Don't misunderstand me, I'm not saying it's always like that. Sometimes the worship is thrilling, the sense of God overwhelming, the experience of communion with him profound and real. Sometimes all distractions are banished. Christ is centre-stage. And I believe, and trust, and yearn, and rejoice. But what I am saying is that times like that are not the only moments of grace. Mysteriously God can and does also act when I am half-hearted, half-believing, half-uninterested, half-concentrating, providing I can produce just enough faith or staying power or openness to him, whatever it is, to respond to that least complicated of all his invitations: 'Come and eat'.

And always it is bread on the menu. Why?

It is bread he invites us to eat because, in the providence of God, the bread is the body of Christ, corpus Christi. It is ridiculously simple, yet deeply mysterious, this idea that, when we Christians look up to heaven and give thanks and call down the Holy Spirit, as we shall do again this evening, God responds by making the presence of Christ real in the bread on the altar. Ridiculously simple, deeply mysterious, and Christian experience has verified it, has found it to be true. The bread is the body of Christ. Don't press me on how precisely. When Christians struggle too hard to explain the how, a beautiful mystery becomes a theological controversy. Accept it as a lovely hardly fathomable truth. Explore it over the years. But long before you've made sense of it, you'll discover it's true. But only if you keep responding to the invitation week by week: 'Come and eat'.

It is the bread of the broken that he invites us to eat. That too is part of the mystery. It is the bread of the broken at more than one level. Bread is broken in order that it may be shared. The invitation to come and eat, though it is deeply personal and addressed to you individually, is never addressed to you alone. It is always an invitation to all who are willing to hear and respond to it. It is always an invitation to a communal meal, to share the bread, and in sharing to make discoveries. It is broken bread because the Eucharist is always rooted in the brokenness of Christ, the Lamb of God, Agnus Dei, who takes away the sins of the world, who allows himself to be broken that God's salvation may be shared. The Eucharist keeps us in touch with the brokenness of Christ and of the world.

But it is also the bread of the broken because it is spiritual food for human beings who are breaking, for human beings who have been broken by suffering, or sin, or setback. Of course there is a long tradition of preparing carefully for communion, of refraining from communion, when things have gone wrong in relationship with God. And I can make sense of that, but it does sometimes lead to people thinking themselves unworthy to receive, staying away from communion when they ought to be coming to the source of healing and peace. The sacraments are for sinners. The worse the mess you're in, the more fragile or broken your life, your faith, your promises, your sanity, the more you need to hear the invitation 'Come and eat'. And when you find yourself at the altar surrounded by people who seem a little mad, or sometimes you suspect rather bad, and certainly lost, and not always adequate, as the world sees it, remember that's the way it's meant to be. This is bread for sinners. This is the place for forgiveness and of healing. Jesus ate with sinners, the Gospels tell us, and nothing changes, for he still enjoys that more than dinner parties with the virtuous. So, come what may, if all else around you is going wrong, keep an ear open for the invitation, and come and eat the bread of brokenness.

Come and eat, for it is also bread of angels. I love that little phrase from Psalm 78. 'He gave them manna to eat. So on earth we share the bread of angels.' That's another part of the many-sided wonder of the Eucharist. It is a chance to play at heaven. It is an invitation to simulate a heavenly party. Heaven is larger than this life, of that I'm sure, and full of love and laughter and song and, though sin gets in the way, the Eucharist is the attempt to anticipate it, to grasp its reality for a moment. Of course most of our Eucharists are fairly earthbound, but not always, and they need not be so. Just occasionally you get a glimpse. It may be the music that lifts you, or the silence, or the affection for one another, or the corporate prayerfulness, or it may be just the sense that the eating and drinking is a pale imitation of a heavenly feast. Just occasionally I hope you have this sense that you are handling the bread of angels. It only happens if you are searching for it, wanting it. Heaven, even a glimpse of heaven, is only for those who are open to its possibilities. So come and eat, and expect the angels on the guest list, and the saints as well.

Bread made body,
bread of brokenness,
bread of angels
bread of life.

Bread of life. That's the last truth to get hold of. Jesus talks about himself as living bread, bread of life. The invitation to come and eat is more than an invitation to a meal; it is an invitation to enter a relationship. For to sit down with Christ, to eat with him and share with him, to have fellowship with him, is to be put in touch with his life-giving, life-sustaining, life-affirming Spirit. It is to have life, and to have it in all its fullness. When I respond to the invitation to come and eat the bread of life, I am responding to an invitation to meet the one who will sit me down and serve me, and then will eat with me, sharing not only his food, but his own very self:

> Behold, I stand at the door and knock. If you hear my voice and open the door, I will come in to you and eat with you, and you with me. (Rev. 3.20)

So, week by week, hear and respond to the invitation to come and eat. It may always be bread on the menu, and not much else, but the bread is for the broken, the bread is the bread of angels, the living bread, the body of Christ. A little piece of bread that looks as if it might blow away. But here, in the providence of God, is the meeting place of death and resurrection, of tears and laughter, of God and humankind. Come and eat. Whatever else you neglect to do, don't fail to come and eat.

Ordination of Deacons

You have come here today to see [some among us] be 'ordained'. Immediately we're into a church-sounding word. To ordain is to admit someone to an 'order', to give them a new kind of belonging. It doesn't detract from the belongings they have already. Still they belong within a family, just as they always have done, and in many cases it is family that has been the principal source of encouragement and support that has brought them to this day. Still they belong to that great Christian family, the whole body of baptized believers, part of what technically is called the *laos*, the company of the people of God. From it we get the word 'laity' and still they are part of that. And there will be other lesser senses of belonging that are not fundamentally changed by what is to happen this morning.

They will still belong to you. And it isn't that today they suddenly belong to God, for they have always belonged to him, even when they didn't know it. But today they become a member of an order, a college if you like, of people committed to the same ministry as themselves, and from that new belonging will come blessings for them and encouragement and support in the years ahead.

It is the order of – what? They are ordained as – what? Well, you know the answer. It's there on the front of the service book. It is the order of deacons to which they are to be joined. It is as a deacon that each will walk out of the cathedral today. 'Send down the Holy Spirit upon your servant for the office and work of a deacon in your Church', the Bishop will say as we all pray fervently and joyfully for each in turn.

But it may be a surprising answer. For I'm almost sure I have never told you that they've been training to be a deacon. Some people may have said to them, 'So you're going into the Church, are you?' They've probably been too polite to say, 'No. I've been in the Church since my baptism', but they have. 'So you're going to be a reverend?' Well, not exactly, though maybe you've noticed them growing more reverend every day! Or maybe not! 'You're going to be a vicar?' Yes, probably, in about four years' time, but not just yet, at least not technically, though you can be quite sure if they walk down the street tomorrow with shiny new white collars they'll be greeted with 'Hello, Vicar' and it's best to answer cheerily and accept the title and not try to explain the subtleties! 'You're going to be a curate.' *Got it.* You're going to be a curate, a minister who shares with another more senior experienced minister in serving the people of the parish and encouraging the ministry there. That's the job you're going to do. But still the service says 'the order of deacons'. And that's true also.

And, if you can make sense of this distinction, a deacon is what they are going to *be* and a curate is what they are going to *do*. One is about the kind of minister they are to be; the other is the title of the job. Today they enter the order of deacons and, whatever lies ahead – priest, vicar, Dean of Derby, Archbishop of Canterbury – they will still be part of the order of deacons. So what is this deacon thing that gives character to their ministry?

You can see something of the origins in Acts chapter 6:

And the twelve called together the whole community of the disciples and said, 'It is not right that we should neglect the word of God in order to wait at tables. Therefore, friends, select from among yourselves seven men of good standing, full of the Spirit and of wisdom, whom we may appoint to this task ... What they said pleased the whole community, and they chose Stephen ... Philip, Prochorus, Nicanor, Timon, Parmenas, and Nicolaus ... They had these men stand before the apostles, who prayed and laid their hands on them. (Acts 6.2–6)

The beginnings of Christian ordained ministry are not very clear, but out of this beginning emerges an order of deacons. Today we also have seven men of good standing, but we have two women of good standing too! The word 'deacon', *diakonos*, means 'servant'. They are entrusted with a ministry of service, of servanthood. 'Waiting on tables' said the apostles. We give them today a 'waiting on tables' ministry. A little later some of them, newly ordained, will do exactly that, lay the table with bread and wine, and all of them serve you when you come to receive communion.

Of course, there is another story we have heard this morning that takes the idea of servanthood somewhat deeper. It is that Gospel reading from John when Jesus, the Lord and Master, gets down on his knees and washes the feet of his disciples and dries them with the towel, telling them incidentally to do the same to one another, as happens here and in thousands of churches each year on Maundy Thursday night. 'If I, your Lord and Master, have washed your feet, you ought also to wash one another's feet.' It's a picture of servanthood that goes beyond waiting at table. It's down on your knees looking up at people, looking up at them from the ground. Jesus, with his towel wrapped around him, the servant. He was of course the Master too, the Servant-King of whom we sing; but it was his serving that gave character to his kingship, showed us what kind of master he was.

There's more, in fact, that comes out of that story than simply the picture of Jesus the Deacon, Jesus the Servant. It does teach us about service, how it is at the heart of ministry, and that's a lesson worth learning. It also teaches us about humility; there's a willingness to embrace the menial task, there's a lack of grandeur, there's what the apostle Paul calls a 'self-emptying'.

Do you remember how he puts it in that wonderful passage in Philippians?

> *Christ Jesus, who, though he was in the form of God, did not regard equality with God as something to be exploited, but emptied himself, taking the form of a slave, being born in human likeness. And being found in human form, he humbled himself and became obedient to the point of death.* (Phil. 2.6–8)

To learn humility, that's part of the calling of the ordained minister. There's such a lot that can push you the other way. It's a crucial lesson to learn, to have the same humility as Christ. The story also teaches us about relationships and how they need to be governed by openness and love. The action of Jesus in washing the disciples' feet has nothing of the solemn ecclesiastical ritual about it. It comes over as a spontaneous, generous, slightly over-the-top bit of affectionate loving, clearly embarrassing at first for the disciples, but actually touching everyone very deeply. It was a wonderful bit of pastoring; it was love acted out and made real.

All that is in the story of Jesus the Deacon: service, certainly; humility, yes; and good relationships characterized by openness and love. And that's what we entrust today to these candidates. A ministry of service, humility and love. Why do we entrust this particular ministry to them today? Two reasons. First, that they may learn those characteristics and those skills that are fundamental to Christ-like ministry, before ever they are entrusted with other responsibilities that speak more of authority and of oversight, so that service, humility and love in ministry become second nature to them and stay with them through all the years that lie ahead. They are key attributes for a minister in pastoral ministry and they are the focus for the months to come – before they return here to be ordained priest.

But we entrust this ministry to them not only for their sake and for the sake of Christ's gospel, but for your sake also – and mine. Orders of ministry exist in part to model for all of us the calling we share. We sometimes say that the Church has an order of priests to help the whole Church; every Christian, to get hold of their calling to be part of Christ's royal priesthood. They help us identify priesthood so that we may try to assimilate it in our own discipleship. So too with deacons. We are all called to servanthood. We are all called to emulate the Servant King. We need some people who will model that for us, keep it before us. Bishops and deans and canons and people like that need it particularly, need to be reminded that inside them is a deacon too and still, years on from their ordination, they're in the business of service, humility and love. But it isn't just them – every one of us needs to have held before us models of Christ-like servanthood. These candidates will offer us that through the next year.

All that is true and important – and just a bit too neat! These nine are going to wait at table and wash feet, metaphorically, and it will be an important part of their ministerial formation. But it isn't going to be all like that, even this year. This neat solution was already going wrong by Acts chapter 7. The first one of the seven to break ranks was Stephen. He was chosen to wait at table, but once the Holy Spirit got hold of him, as we are going to pray that the Holy Spirit will get hold of these nine today, he started preaching, preaching powerfully, doing the very same thing the apostles wanted to be set free to do themselves, proclaiming the word of God. 'Stephen, full of grace and power,' the writer tells us, 'did great wonders and signs among the people'. Whether he went on taking his turn on the table-waiting rota is not revealed, but I hope he did, for we do honour him as the first deacon, as well as the first martyr – yes, that is where it led.

Filled with the Holy Spirit, Stephen found that he had to share the good news of Jesus Christ. He had to speak out about what God had done. He had to proclaim the gospel. And that has always been part of the ministry of deacons too – whether in the liturgy itself or in the life of the Christian community or out on the boundaries engaging with the non-Christian world and proclaiming the gospel. Of course, that's not in contradiction to the ministry of servanthood. The gospel is powerfully commended by those actions that show Christians serving the world, washing the bruised limbs of broken humanity. The gospel is wonderfully proclaimed by every act of service, every sign of genuine humility, and by every generous act of loving. Actions speak louder than words often – but not *always*, and the deacon is given gifts of the Spirit to speak, to proclaim, to tell, to challenge, to evangelize. Thus it is that, as we send them out at the end of the service, we equip them for this new ministry by giving them the Christian Scriptures, the tool of the deacon's trade, the good news of God in Christ the Servant King. By it, the deacon is to live and to grow into conformity with Christ. By it, the deacon is to share the faith with grace and power. Listen, all of you, to what the Spirit leads them to say. Through them God will be speaking to you.

Within the order of deacons, men and women are drawn into holy things. They are given the space to study the Scriptures, to worship and to pray every day in company with colleagues. They stand close to the priest in the celebration of the sacraments and capture, please God, something of the beauty of holiness that shines through worship that is in spirit and in truth. In some of their pastoral encounters they will discover in the people they meet goodness, holiness and faith that seems to be very much in touch with heaven. A sense of the sheer marvel of God and the unutterable beauty of the Lord, responding with a sense of unworthiness and humility:

> *Woe is me! I am lost, for I am a man of unclean lips ... yet my eyes have seen the King, the* LORD *of hosts.* (Isa. 6.5)

But God had a purpose for Isaiah. 'Who shall I send and who will go for us?' he asked. And Isaiah, filled with the vision of heaven, replied 'Send me'. May these new deacons, sensing the divine holiness, accepting the invitation to servant ministry after the pattern of the Servant King, find themselves saying, over and over again, 'Send me'. Continuing to model for us all Christian service, Christ-like humility and divine love, may they, like Stephen, be full of the grace and power of the Holy Spirit and confident in the proclaiming of the gospel. Come, Holy Spirit, come.

Ordination of Priests

It is an Easter story, and it is the risen Lord who is speaking to us through that story. It is just a small part of the awesome tale of triumph that the evangelists tell. The Lord has gone, willingly, resolutely, to the cross and his body has been laid in the tomb. But then comes Easter Day, and that event that is at the heart of faith and at the heart of the vocation of these 11 men and women here today who come ready to be admitted to the order of priests. The Lord returns. The Lord is risen. The Lord has new things to say and fresh things to do. This afternoon we hear about the way he came to them in the upper room on the first evening, but see that within its wider context – the Lord who appears to Mary Magdalene in the garden and calls her by her name; the Lord who falls in step with disciples on a journey and then reveals who he is, their risen Lord, as he breaks the bread with them; the Lord who summons the fishermen-disciples to breakfast on the lakeside; the Lord who faces Simon Peter with his denial, three times asks whether Peter loves him, and commissions him to feed the sheep; the Lord who takes them to the hill-top, gives them the Great Commission, and assures them that he will be with them to the end of time. That is the context in which he comes and stands among them in the upper room, says to them 'Peace be with you', shows them his hands and his side, and breathes on them that they might be sent out with authority in the power of the Spirit.

There is such a lot to give thanks for today.

There is the evidence here before us that the Church of Christ is – despite the prophets of despair and misrepresentation – in good heart, able to inspire lively men and women to give their lives to its service and to the service of Christ as deacons and as priests, playing their part in that process whereby we shall gradually reverse the decline in numbers of ordained ministers that had overtaken us.

There is the faith and love, sacrifice and staying power that has brought these 11 to this moment. And it is not all their faith and love, sacrifice and staying power, though praise the Lord for that. It is the faith and love and sacrifice and staying power of parents, of husband or wife, of children, of friends, of sending churches – and wonderful it is that all those are represented here today.

There is the growth in ministry of these 11 over the last 12 months since last they knelt here to be made deacons, crossing a threshold that will have changed them in ways that will have surprised them. That they are here again today is a tribute to family, to colleagues, to parishioners, to those among whom they have ministered. They have come back because, working alongside you, sharing the work of ministry that is yours too, their vocation has been confirmed, their desire to serve Jesus Christ in the priesthood of his Church strengthened.

For all that we give thanks but, more than all that, and making sense of all that, we give thanks because today, as so often if we will open our eyes to see and our ears to hear, the risen Lord is among us. He has come to stand among us, though in truth he is never far away. He says *today* to those who will hear, 'Peace be with *you*'. He shows *us* his hands and his side. And he breathes upon *us*. That's what is going on this afternoon and our response is a deep thankfulness, but also a real sense of awe and a profound longing. At least I pray that may be true: in each one of us, different as we are, deep thankfulness, a real sense of awe and a profound longing. Spend a few minutes with me, reflecting on that upper room story and its impact on us today, and on these 11 men and women ministering within the body of Christ in the years to come.

He has come to stand among us. He is the Lord to whom we have sung already: 'Glory to you, O Lord', 'Praise to you, O Christ'. We have addressed him because he is here. That's the point of the resurrection faith. We do not have a Lord who simply 'was', once upon a time. We have a Lord who 'is', and will be to the end of time and beyond even that. He is here in the assembly of his people. He is here in the Scriptures that we have read and on which we reflect. He is here when we take the bread and the wine, give thanks, break and receive. Once again, as always unfailingly, if only we will perceive it, he will be known to us, and will touch us, in the breaking of the bread, like it was at supper at Emmaus and at breakfast on the lakeside.

And that's good news for these candidates, for it means that, wherever their ministry leads them, they can know that Jesus is with them. With them for their own sake, but with them also for the sake of others. They can know that where they are, trying to be faithful, trying to show him forth, Jesus will be in them, through them and by them making himself available to those among whom they minister. *They* will sense the presence of the Lord, as we do today, but in their faithful ministry *others* will sense the presence of the Lord, providing that as the years go by they go on seeking to be conformed to the pattern of Christ.

His first words are 'Peace be with you'. To disciples in an upper room, they were absolutely the right words with which to begin, for they were in turmoil, both because the Lord had been put to death and buried in a tomb, but also because the body had gone and there were stories of an earthquake, an angel, a gardener and probably more. Into that turmoil, as into a storm that needs to be stilled, comes the word of assurance, 'Peace be with you'. The word of assurance, the message that restores, heals, makes whole. We look a happy lot today – though Anglicans hardly ever manage to look as wonderfully over-the-top joyful as we often have reason to be, but we do look a fairly happy lot! But, among us, of course (it could not be otherwise), there will be those for whom life just now means turmoil – worry, doubt, pain, stress. Jesus says to you, 'Peace be with you'. And in that word of calm he wants to begin with you a relationship in which there can be love and healing and joy too. He calls you by your name, as he did Mary on the resurrection day. He calls you back to himself and invites your love, as he offers you his, as he did to Simon Peter after that lakeside breakfast. He wants to give you his peace.

And that's good news for all these candidates, for he says *this* to them. If, among all the joy of today there's any sense of inadequacy or trepidation, he says it to them *today*. And if, much later on, there is a time when it all looks in danger of falling apart, he'll say it to them *then*. So they must always be listening. Today, the Bishop speaks to each their name in the ordination prayer. But it is the Lord who, at a deeper level, will call them by their name, for each is uniquely precious to him. When they make a mess of things, as sometimes they certainly will, he will not reprove, but ask them again, 'Do you love me?', and send them back to tending the sheep, because he doesn't give up on people whom he has chosen. He doesn't give up on loving them. He doesn't give up on asking for their love and their service. But part of what he will entrust to them is the task of saying, in a thousand different contexts, where there is human need, 'Peace be with you'. They are to be his peace-makers. They are to be instruments of his healing, his reconciliation, his wholeness. 'Whoever's sins you forgive, they are forgiven' he says to the disciples, and that is awesome authority entrusted to the Church working through its ministers. But it's just *part* of the ministry of peace-maker, helping God's peace get through to still the turmoil in the human soul. 'Peace be with you', he says to them today, that they may be instruments of his peace.

And then he shows them his hands and his side. This wonderful, glorious, victorious risen Lord is also the man of scars. Even on Easter Day they need to engage with the wounds. In his hands, the holes made by the nails. The man of scars with a message of peace for a broken humanity. In the ordination prayer, the new priests hold out their hands and the Bishop makes with the oil of chrism the sign of the cross on their palms. The oil speaks of the anointing of the Holy Spirit; it is a sign of divine empowering. The hands are the hands that will bless, absolve, touch, heal in the name of Christ. But they are going to be marked with a cross. It is a reminder of the nails. The Lord who is among us now is the man of scars.

And that's important for those about to be ordained priest. I believe it is good news for them, though, to be honest, it is a difficult bit of good news and it can take a lifetime to recognize that it is such. For it is a reminder that the way of the Christian is always the way of the cross and those who commit themselves to a tough path of discipleship (and ordained ministry certainly is that) must expect sometimes to tread a path of hurt, of rejection, of humiliation and of pain. It isn't going to be fun all the way. It wasn't fun all the way for Jesus. It is a wonderful vocation, but it involves sacrifice. Expectations of clergy can be quite unreasonable, the world can scoff, and church-people be wickedly cruel. You can raise your hand to bless people and they all but curse you. And sometimes you can be just so tired, you wonder whether there isn't a better way (and there probably is). There will be scars. But, remember, they belong to the glorious risen Lord, who has come through, stands with you, and says, 'Peace be with you'. Remember that, all of you, when you see these priests exercising the immense privilege the Church gives them to stand at the altar-table and preside when the people of God gather to meet the Lord in word and sacrament at Holy Communion. For there they, we, show his death, his scars, his broken body, yet celebrate his resurrection and partake of his risen life. The one who presides at the Eucharist has to carry the cross joyfully in their soul.

And then he breathes on them. It is the breath of the Holy Spirit. He makes that explicit. 'Receive the Holy Spirit' he says as he breathes on them. And, 'As the Father has sent me, even so I send you.' He is with them, he assures them with his message of peace, he shows them his scars and then he empowers them. He sends them and equips them with the Spirit that they may be effective in his service. It is a kind of Pentecost, and that is good news for Jonathan, Edward and the others. For the Holy Spirit features largely in what we do today and what lies beyond. As we all pray from the heart for these 11 in turn, the Bishop will call upon the Father and say: 'Send down the Holy Spirit upon your servant' – Gill, Pip, Andrew and the others. And both parts of what the Lord said on Easter evening are there, the sending and the Spirit. It is the Spirit that was first called down upon you in your baptism. The same Spirit that came upon Mary at the annunciation. The same Spirit that came at Pentecost. The same Spirit that the priest, speaking for the people, asks the Father to send down in every Eucharist that we may be renewed and fed. The same Spirit who will be called down upon every new Christian whom these new priests will baptize in the name of the Church. That same Spirit who comes today in response to our prayers, anointing these 11 for the office and work of a priest, will dwell within them to develop within them the gifts they need to 'equip the saints for the work of ministry, for building up the body of Christ'. Today, rather dramatically, a moment of divine power. Tomorrow, the next day, and always, the quiet refreshing, renewing, anointing Spirit, if they will be open to receive.

This is an Easter event. The risen Lord stands among us. 'Peace be with you' he says. He shows the scars. He breathes upon his chosen servants. Come, Holy Spirit, come.

Seventh Sunday after Trinity, Proper 12, Year C

'Jesus was praying in a certain place, after he had finished, one of his disciples said to him, "Lord, teach us to pray."' So begins today's Gospel reading from the eleventh chapter of St Luke's Gospel.

Today is a really good day for me. It is my first service in the Forest since becoming bishop – not my first trip into the Forest, but my first service, and I am glad about that. It is being celebrated with you in St John's Cinderford, and I'm glad about that too, and I thank you for your welcome. And just to make it an even better day, we have just heard that Gospel reading, which gives me every reason to preach about prayer. Preaching about prayer is something I am always pleased to do, because I do believe prayer to be absolutely vital and central to the Church's life and ministry. I would rather be a bishop who talks about prayer, is known to take prayer seriously and encourages people in the life of prayer, than be a bishop known for clever strategies and new initiatives (though they have their place too).

I once got a headline in *The Times* because of something I said in a lecture. 'Anglicans have lost the art of prayer, says canon' was the headline. I was the canon. The phone rang all day, whether people who agreed (on the basis of the headline; most of them didn't read more than that) or disagreed. What the 'canon' had actually said was that the Church needed to recover the art of praying the liturgy, and that's not quite the same. But I think there was some truth in the headline, even if I hadn't quite said it.

'Anglicans have lost the art of prayer.' 'One of the disciples of Jesus said to him, "Lord, teach us to pray."' Let's explore this a bit more. For I do believe that the key to the renewal of worship, whether here or anywhere else, is the prayerfulness of the congregation. It isn't new words, or modern music, or fancy movements or even rich symbolism that make worship a deep encounter with God, but a spirit of prayer permeating the liturgy from beginning to end.

This is how it works. Not every stage of the service is labelled 'Prayer'. There are other things too: readings, sermon, creed, peace, communion, dismissal, etc. But at various points there is prayer. Classically there is prayer near the beginning – the collect; prayer in the middle – intercession, and later thanksgiving; and prayer near the end – another collect after communion. And the word 'collect' is itself a strong hint of what is supposed to be going on. For a collect is the prayer the president says to collect up, to gather up, the prayers, usually silent, of the whole community of worshippers. And, because you can hardly collect up what hasn't had time to happen, the collect has to come after a space, often of silence, in which people are having the chance to pray. The intercession is also like that – part agenda-setting by the leader, part-prayer by the people.

Now those are the points where prayer is on the surface – everyone conscious of it and sharing in it to the extent that they are able. But what happens to it in between through all the rest of the service? What happens to it when the Scriptures are being read, or the sermon preached, or the peace exchanged, or an anthem sung? If it has simply stopped, that is when the worship fails as the prayerfulness evaporates. No, what needs to happen is that it needs to continue, but to go underground. Prayer goes on, almost subconsciously, as people keep it going in their hearts as we do all those other things. This is the pattern we need to work for – a prayerfulness from beginning to end, most of the time quietly below the surface, but sometimes coming up to that surface to be renewed.

The effect of that, of course, is not just a prayerful liturgy that touches deeply not only the faithful, but also any casual visitor, but also that every individual part of the service is transformed. The Scripture readings that are being prayed, as well as heard being read, make their impact in a new way. The greeting of peace that is being prayed takes on a deeper character than one that is just a jolly hand-shaking. The sharing of communion that is being prayed is going to draw communicants into an experience of the living God in a way that the surface activity of receiving can never do alone. The anthem that is prayed both by those who sing it and those who listen to it is transformed from performance into prayer.

The message is straightforward. If there's a gap, fill it with prayer. When prayer comes to the surface, use it well, so that when it goes underground you can carry it on, albeit unconsciously, through every other element of the rite.

But that's only the beginning. If we all tried to make sense of that, and worked at that, we should have a Spirit-filled prayerful liturgy. But what we want and need is more than that: we want Spirit-filled prayerful lives. After all, we come to church on Sundays partly to be resourced. We want to go away each week better equipped for the week ahead with all its opportunities, tensions, humdrum boredom or frenetic activity. And we are resourced in a variety of ways. On a good Sunday the sermon might help! The warmth and friendship may strengthen us. The music may inspire. Certainly the sacrament itself will renew us. But I suspect that one of the richest and most precious things we can receive is the art of, and the inclination to, prayerfulness. The ability to pray through the week is crucial if we are to stay close to Christ and rise above the challenges of daily living.

And part of the function of the Sunday liturgy is to train us for daily living. If here each Sunday you learn to pray both on the surface consciously and below the surface less consciously, you may be enabled to acquire the same pattern in your daily lives, so that you approach that also through moments of conscious surface prayer – traditionally first thing in the morning and last thing at night, though not necessarily then – that go underground but enable you to pray your way through life, with a gentleness and peace and confidence that are all too rare. If that's right, and I'm sure it is, we work away at praying the liturgy, not just because, to put it crudely, it makes a good service, but also because it makes for a better life.

But, to come down to earth, we have to be honest and say that most of us are not very good at it. We are still, most of us, in the reception class of the school of prayer. To be left to our own prayerful devices from Monday to Saturday gives us an independence with which we cannot profitably cope. And that's why the tradition of weekday worship, which churches like this have been particularly strong on, is very important and crucial to maintain – the offering of the Eucharist by the priest and those who, as opportunity occurs, join with him to make a small community of people praying together and exploring other opportunities.

Not everyone, of course, is in a position to be part of such a community, at least not often, but the pattern of daily worship is there simply to encourage. Not everyone can be physically present, but everyone can be encouraged by the knowledge that such prayer goes on. It can strengthen them to persevere with prayer at home and with a prayerful approach to daily living. Those who gather to pray, whether in church or in homes, do so not only for themselves but for the whole community. There is a special responsibility laid on those who can come to pray to do so in order to strengthen those who cannot because of the constraints of their daily life.

So, when we pray, whether it be the praying that is the undercurrent of the liturgy, or the extension of that praying that goes on in daily living, how do we pray? The key may be to have lots of space and the art of filling it with prayer, but what kind of prayer? Jesus' response to that question was what we have come to call 'the Lord's Prayer'. 'When you pray, say: Father, hallowed be your name ...' and so on. Luke, in today's Gospel, gives us a short version; it is Matthew who fills it out. Legion are the sermons people preach about the Lord's Prayer. Sermon courses can go on for weeks taking a line at a time, and it's a profitable exercise. People find a marvellous pattern to it all, so that it becomes a model for all good praying. I'm never quite convinced, and some of the patterns seem a bit artificial to me.

To be honest, what strikes me about the Lord's Prayer is its arbitrariness. All sorts of things come out, in an order that doesn't look to me as if it is irreversible – hallowed be your name, your kingdom come, give us bread, forgive our sins, save us from the time of trial. You could turn the order round and nothing is very different. And the other thing that strikes me is that no idea is developed much. You've only just mentioned one thing and you're on to another. And the conclusion that I draw from this is that, far from giving us a model prayer, Jesus is saying something like this: When you pray, just let it come. Just get talking to the Father. Don't plan the conversation. Don't remind yourself, rather like an old-fashioned prayer manual, to start with adoration, and don't forget confession, and prayer for others before yourself. For conversations aren't structured neatly like that. Just start conversing with the Father, and listening too. Just tell God things, and ask God things, and don't worry about shape and form. Communication is all that matters – communication, relationship. If that's authentic, there's prayer being offered at a deep level. The liturgy with its own deep structures will hold the shape. Just fill the silences with natural communication with the Father, speaking and listening, though not a word be heard.

You can learn that also from our first reading this morning from the Book of Genesis. What is there described is Abraham's prayer to God by the oaks at Mamre in which he begs God not to destroy the cities of Sodom and Gomorrah lest there be innocent people there who will perish with the guilty. But did you hear it as Abraham saying his prayers? Was it not much more like Abraham engaged in a conversation with God? And so it should have been, for authentic prayer is like that – genuine communication, real conversation – though yes, of course, sometimes we are reduced to contemplative silence, with conversation falling away, when faced with the sheer holiness of God.

What the Church desperately needs, for the world's sake, is people who talk to God and listen too, naturally, spontaneously, sometimes excitedly, in the liturgy, so that the presence of God here is overwhelming and real and almost tangible. People, who having developed that art and that discipline (for it is both) within the liturgy find it spills over into prayer at home and prayer in the events of every day. Isn't that worth working at?

Lord, teach us to pray, as you taught your disciples.

St Peter's Day

Where do we begin with Peter? With so many of the saints there is so little to say with certainty. Even some of those in the Scriptures are little more than names. You could put on a postcard what we know about Philip and Bartholomew and Phoebe. Even some of the later saints are clothed in mystery and myth. That doesn't matter much, for the most important truth about the saints is that, alive in God's presence, they are united with us in a communion of prayer and praise. I don't need to know much about somebody to pray and praise alongside them.

But Peter! There is so much to know. Peter, with three different versions of his call in three Gospels, Peter the fisherman, Peter who attempted to walk on the water, Peter who witnessed the transfiguration and the agony of Christ in the garden, Peter who was reluctant to let Jesus wash his feet, Peter who messed up mightily in his denial of Jesus, Peter who ran to the tomb, Peter who preached with power on the day of Pentecost, Peter who went to the Gentiles, Peter who raised Tabitha from death, Peter who went to Rome and died there for Christ, Peter who gave his name to two of the books of the New Testament. A wealth of stories, revealing to us an attractive follower of Christ, but more than that, one who became his friend. You could write a book about Peter!

But this evening I want to focus on just three Peter stories and on two key words Jesus spoke to him. Let's begin with that passage from Acts 12. Peter, imprisoned when the persecutions begin, is miraculously rescued from his cell by the ministry of an angel. To start with, he thinks he must be dreaming. This just can't be real. But then the angel disappears and Peter finds himself standing on the right side of the prison gates, a free man. 'Now I am sure that the Lord has sent me his angel and rescued me from the hands of Herod and from all that the Jewish people are expecting.' Of course, the lectionary cut us short. The story goes on and becomes almost farce-like when Peter knocks on the door of the house where the Christian community is gathered praying for him, and the maid who comes to the door is so excited when she sees him that she goes off to tell the others, leaving Peter on the pavement. It's a lovely human detail. But from that story learn this. Peter understands here, as he does elsewhere, the wonderful power of God. Learns it, maybe only begins to understand it. 'The Lord has sent his angel and rescued me.' There were other occasions, of course, when he saw the wonderful power of God – when Jesus walked on the water, even if Peter's faith failed in the middle of that story, when Jesus stilled the storm, when Jesus turned water into wine at the wedding banquet, when Jesus was bathed in light and the voice spoke from heaven on the holy mountain, when Peter found the tomb empty on Easter Day, when the Holy Spirit on the Day of Pentecost made him amazingly articulate in speaking of Jesus. The wonderful power of God and here it was to enable his escape from prison.

There's something for us to contemplate. Like Peter, we should strive to know, even to understand, the wonderful power of God. We should try to understand it as it is manifested in those stories in the Scriptures. But also we should try to understand it in our contemporary world. The wonderful things God does in our own times, within the Church and beyond it, the wonderful power of God in individual lives, the wonderful power of God in our own lives. This weekend I have ordained eight priests and ten deacons. Each of them can tell extraordinarily encouraging stories of how the power of God has been at work in their lives that has brought them to this day. And you, if you will stop long enough to think, can tell stories of how God has acted powerfully in your lives. And it's good not only to know and to understand, but also to tell.

Understand the wonderful power of God. We're quite a long way into the ministry of Jesus. Peter and the other disciples have been around quite a long time. In fact we are not far off from the point when that ministry changes from that of an itinerant preacher and healer into the purposeful journey of a man who understands his destiny and sets his face steadfastly towards Jerusalem. But first will come the transfiguration and, just before that, this event we heard about this evening at Caesarea Philippi. 'Whom do you say I am?' And Peter, as so often ready to jump in, the spokesman of the group, comes out with a profound truth. 'You are the Messiah' – the Christ, the Anointed One – and he adds, 'the Son of the Living God'. It's not the first time some of them have said this. Some of them found themselves recognizing Jesus as the Son of God when he walked on the water. But Peter hadn't been part of that – he was shivering in the boat having had to be rescued by Jesus from the water. But it is his moment and he rises to the occasion and comes out with this perfect affirmation of faith in who this Jesus was and is. He has a conviction about who Jesus is. Here is someone much more than a preacher and a healer, more than a miracle worker. Here is God's Anointed, God's Son. And Jesus responds, 'Blessed are you, Simon son of Jonah.' It is the only time Jesus says this – 'Blessed are you' – of anyone and it is to Peter that he says it. 'Blessed are you, Simon son of Jonah! For flesh and blood has not revealed this to you, but my Father in heaven. And I tell you, you are Peter, the Rock, and on this rock I will build my church.'

He has a conviction about who Jesus is. That is also something for you and me. There are people who have no time for Jesus. But there are many others for whom he is a figure they revere. He is a holy man, a teacher, an exemplar of ethical living. But Christianity says so much about him. He is Emmanuel, God with us, God incarnate. He is Saviour, he is the Christ, the Anointed One. To have seen Jesus is to have met with God. He is the human face of God. He is God's Son. 'If you have seen me, you have seen the Father', Jesus himself says. And that is what is asked of us, to recognize Jesus for who he really is and to share that incredibly good news with those around us.

For that is what Peter did. Maybe he was slow to begin. Maybe he fell from grace. But from a day in Eastertide by the sea of Tiberias and a day called Pentecost in the city of Jerusalem, consistently and courageously, he told people who this Jesus was and is and invited them to put their faith in Jesus. And the Acts of the Apostles shows him doing that to great effect and the Letters of Peter witness to that faith in Jesus.

He understands the wonderful power of God. He has a conviction about who Jesus is. Third, he knows himself forgiven and loved. The story, of course, is that in John 21, on the shore of the lake. The disciples, Peter in the lead as usual, have been fishing all night and have caught nothing. Dawn breaks and there is Jesus on the shore cooking the breakfast. 'Come and eat', he says. They are full of joy because it is the Lord. But there is some unfinished business. For Peter is covered in shame for his denial – three-times denial – of Jesus on the night Jesus died, and that needs sorting. 'Simon, son of John, do you love me?' asks Jesus – not once, but three times. 'You know I love you', says Peter – not once, but three times. Three denials to be cancelled, not so much with faith as with love.

To understand the wonderful power of God – that is amazing! To have a conviction about who Jesus is – that's a beautiful truth! But to know yourself forgiven and loved. What Peter needed more than else. It is what Jesus wanted to say to him more than anything else. And Peter never looked back – the impetuous Peter who often seemed to get it wrong is replaced by a Peter who is the confident leader of the post-resurrection community. He is indeed the rock on which Christ builds the Church. Peter, once he is assured of love, can flourish in himself and for the gospel.

And so with us. We need to know for ourselves the forgiveness and love that is on offer through Jesus. It is an overflowing love that comes from within the mystery of the Trinity – the Father loving the Son, the Son loving the Father, the Spirit the love flowing between them – and it is on offer to you and to me. And given to you and me that we may become agents and instruments of the overflowing love so that it may flow where people have never experienced it before. 'Do you love me?' 'Yes, Lord, you know that I love you.' 'Love one another as I have loved you.'

Peter understands the wonderful power of God. Peter has a conviction about who Jesus is. Peter knows himself forgiven and loved. You, the people of St Peter's Newnham on Severn, understand the wonderful power of God. You, the people of St Peter's Newnham on Severn, have a conviction about who Jesus is. You, the people of St Peter's Newnham on Severn, have a conviction about who Jesus is. You, the people of St Peter's Newnham on Severn, know yourselves forgiven and loved.

And if that is so, hear again the first words that Jesus says to Peter as Matthew tells it and the last words the risen Jesus says to Peter as John tells it – 'Follow me!' It is the call of Jesus to every disciple. It is the call of Jesus to each one of you today. Understanding the wonderful power of God, having a conviction about who we are, knowing ourselves forgiven and loved, follow me!

Mary Magdalene, Macrina
and Margaret

This is going to be a tale of three holy women.

I begin with Mary Magdalene, because it will be her feast day on Tuesday. There are three occasions when we encounter Mary Magdalene in the Gospels. The first is where we are told of a small group of women disciples who were part of the apostolic company and cared for Jesus. We are told that among this group was Mary Magdalene, out of whom the Lord had cast demons. The second is that she is named among those women who were at the foot of the cross on Calvary Hill when the Lord met his death. The third is that she was among the group that went to the tomb before it was light on Easter Day, and that it was she who was the first to encounter the risen Lord, with that compelling exchange and the cry of recognition and of faith: 'Rabbuni, my Master!'

It is important to say that those three mentions of Mary, which add up, of course, to something very significant in the Christian story, is all we know. Tradition has gone further and identified Mary Magdalene with the Mary of the Martha, Mary and Lazarus story and with the Mary who had been a sinner, a prostitute the implication is, who anoints the Lord's feet and dries them with her hair. The Church has sometimes turned Mary into a fallen woman turned penitent. The Church in this case, as so often, means men! But that really is unlikely conjecture.

It's typical, you may think, that Mary Magdalene ends up as chief penitent of the Gospels, whereas in truth she is the first witness of the resurrection. The Eastern Church calls her, and the medieval Church in the West apparently called her, 'the apostle to the apostles' because of her role in the resurrection story. It is a fine title and, whatever you make of the issue of women's ministry in the Church, must make you think. Jesus chose 12 men. Only one was there on Calvary. But all the women were there. And it was to one of the women that Jesus first revealed his resurrection. It makes you think! 'The apostle of the apostles' – that's quite a title!

If we rid ourselves of the image of Mary the Penitent, what do we learn from the authentic stories about her? In a sense to learn anything is to miss the point. That encounter in the garden is not so much about learning something as simply allowing oneself to be thrilled by the sheer wonder of that meeting where the atmosphere is charged with deep emotion and every word has significance. To try to unpack it almost robs it of its power. But, if we are to learn something, let it be this.

God's gift of life and of wholeness is repeatedly on offer. We don't know about the demons that Jesus cast out of Mary before she became a disciple. We don't even talk that sort of language. But we take it to mean that he found her a suffering woman and he made her whole, he restored her to health, he gave her life. And her response was to follow him. Some whom he cured he sent away; others like Mary became part of his company. Made whole, restored to health, given life, she stayed with him until she stood with the mother of the Lord at the foot of the cross and watched as health and wholeness deserted him, and he gave up his life and let death take him over. And for Mary that must have been a return to the darkness she thought she had left behind. In his death her own wholeness and health and life must have seemed to be ebbing away. But God's gift of life and of wholeness is repeatedly on offer and for Mary the miracle happens again. He meets her in the garden and once again makes her whole. Of course it is the first instance of that wonderful Christian truth that those who meet the risen Lord – and he does meet people today as much as then – experience a resurrection in themselves. The resurrection life is for sharing. Jesus does not keep it to himself. Mary is caught up in it and we can be too.

But let me introduce the second holy woman. The Church celebrated her feast day yesterday. She is Macrina. Born in Caesarea, in what is now Turkey, the child of an aristocratic Christian family in the fourth century, she was one of three remarkable siblings. Macrina was the eldest, but then came Basil, destined to be one of the great teachers of the Eastern Church – indeed, called 'Basil the Great', Bishop of Caesarea – and then there was Gregory, who became Bishop of Nyssa. All three were theologians, not just the men, but Macrina too; all three were teachers of the faith. It's typical that Basil and Gregory have been famous through most of Christian history, but Macrina's contribution has been suppressed until very recently. Basil was an academic thinker, Gregory more of a spiritual theologian, Macrina – well, Gregory gives us the flavour of Macrina's faith when he reproduces her dying prayer, spoken in his presence, just before her death in 379. Here it is:

O Lord, you have freed us from the fear of death; you have made the end of life here the beginning of true life for us. For a period you give rest to our bodies in sleep, but then awaken us with the call of the last trumpet. Our earthly body, formed by your hands, you consign in trust to the earth; and then once more you reclaim it, transfiguring with immortality and grace whatever in us is mortal or deformed. You have opened to us the way of resurrection, and given to those who fear you the sign of the holy cross as their emblem, to destroy the enemy and to save our life.

O eternal Lord God, on you have I depended since my mother's womb; you my soul has loved with all its strength; to you I dedicated my body and my soul from childhood. Set by my side an angel of light to lead me to the place of refreshment where there are restful waters in the midst of your holy ones. You have shattered the flaming sword, and in your compassion, you restored the thief who was crucified with you. Let not the terrible abyss of the dead separate me from your chosen ones; let not the accuser bar my way. Forgive me my sins that my soul may be received in your sight, blameless and spotless.

It is a remarkable and beautiful prayer. But I repeat it partly because it has such resonances of the Mary Magdalene story, coincidental as that may be. There is the overall sense of the God who heals, forgives and restores. But, beyond that, there is the echo of Calvary, the Calvary where Mary had stood – 'In your compassion you restored the thief who was crucified with you to paradise. Remember me also in your kingdom, for I too have been crucified with you.' And then that lovely phrase – 'you have opened for us the way to resurrection' – and she continues 'and given to those who fear you the sign of the cross as their emblem, to destroy the enemy and to save our life'. The fourth-century Macrina interprets for us the experience of the first-century Magdalene. Both show us the path that leads via Calvary to the garden of the resurrection.

And then there's Margaret, for today is St Margaret's Day. Today the Church commemorates Margaret, martyr at Antioch in the same century as Macrina lived, the fourth century, though Margaret died, we believe, at the beginning of that century in the Diocletian persecution, but Macrina died near the end. Yesterday Macrina, today Margaret and on Tuesday Mary Magdalene. About Margaret we know almost nothing. There are a whole host of legends, but all of them late and unreliable. All we do know is that the Church at Antioch, which was careful about whom it commemorated, venerated a Christian woman martyr called Margaret or Marina. That's all we know, very little, but in another sense more than enough. For the martyr does not witness by a heroic or holy life, by theological skill or spiritual discipline, by a life story. The martyr witnesses by having such faith and trust in Jesus Christ that he or she is willing to be killed for the sake of Christ – remember Macrina's words ('Remember me also in your kingdom, for I also have been crucified with you') – believing in the eternal life that awaits the chosen ones – Macrina again ('You have opened for us the way to resurrection, and given to those who fear you the sign of the holy cross as their emblem to destroy the enemy and to save our life'). That's all that matters – the cross and the empty tomb that Mary Magdalene discovered, the way to resurrection. And that's the one thing we know about Margaret of Antioch, that she was a martyr for Christ. In their different ways that was all that mattered to Mary, Macrina and Margaret. It ought to be a very large part of what matters to you and to me.

The Feast of the
Blessed Virgin Mary

It is very good to be here celebrating the Feast of the Blessed
Virgin Mary. A wonderful day in a lovely church on an attractive festival celebrating an amazing woman.

The problem with many of the saints is that we know so little
for certain about them – even the majority of those in the New
Testament – that building up a real picture of them in our mind
is difficult. With Mary, of course, the problem is the opposite.
The Gospels tell us much and the Christian tradition has added
more. So many words have been written about her, so many
titles accorded to her, so many pictures painted of her, that it
is hard to find the real Miriam of Nazareth behind the Mary
of the Church. And to add to it, in Christian history we have
even made this wonderful woman, whose song declares that
every generation will call blessed, a figure of controversy and a
source of division. And that's an immense sadness that we must
hope is passing away through ecumenical convergence.

At the risk of adding to the words and the pictures, I want
to explore with you some of the less common ways of speaking of Mary. Leave on one side, as important but not for this
morning/evening, Mary as mother, Mary as virgin, Mary as
the obedient one, Mary as the suffering one and much more.
Explore instead with me these four: Mary as collaborator,
Mary as prophet, Mary as god-bearer, Mary as sister. Collaborator, prophet, god-bearer, sister. Just a little on each, and each
with some application for you and me.

Mary as collaborator. Here I have to take you to the annunciation story, so loved of the artists with fair Gabriel and beautiful Mary visually in dialogue, though the conversation at a deeper level is between the peasant girl and her God. God has a divine purpose. He must come among his people in the person of the Son to be their Saviour. And he has a plan. He will be born as a human baby; he will, as Paul says in his letter to the Galatians, be born of a woman. And how is that going to be? Through the collaboration of Miriam, Mary as we call her, of Nazareth, whom the angel tells us is 'full of grace' even before the Holy Spirit has come upon her and the power of the Most High has overshadowed her. The language of the annunciation story, although it is not exactly the language of invitation and acceptance (in the end God is saying what he wants), has about it the sense of a God who is looking for one who will collaborate with him. Traditionally we speak of Mary's 'I am the handmaid of the Lord. Be it unto me according to your word' as Mary's obedience. But to me her 'yes' is something much more exciting and life-giving than a kind of resigned obedience. It is the yes of the willing collaborator, the co-worker. Perhaps a Mary full of grace was bound to say yes, but in a way I want to cling to the idea of a God who holds his breath waiting and hoping that it will be yes that she says. And he is not disappointed. And so the incarnation comes about through a wonderful partnership of the human and the divine, the Holy Spirit and the Virgin – the initiative God's of course, but the human response vital to the enterprise. And because it was a wonderful partnership of the human and the divine, its fruit was Jesus Christ, truly God and truly a man, utterly and equally human and divine. Mary the collaborator with the Creator.

And I think that is exciting, not only because it is the beginning of the tale of our redemption, but because it gives us a clue to what God is like. He is a collaborative God. He is always on the look-out for partners. When we talk about finding our vocation, it is about discovering not just what God wants us to do with our lives, but what he wants us to do with him in our lives, what form of partnership he wants with each one of us. Maybe, if he is God, he could just do everything himself. Maybe it's not quite orthodox to say God needs you and me, for does God have needs? There's a theological issue for another day. But I have this hunch God just thrives on looking for partners, that he doesn't believe in doing things on his own. I believe he sometimes asks you and me to come on board some grand endeavour or some very modest piece of divine initiative and, yes, with a certain vulnerability our forebears did not recognize, holds his breath and waits for our response. And there are both grand endeavours and modest pieces of divine initiative in God's world today, and in the diocese of Gloucester and in this benefice, just waiting for your joyful 'yes'. Will you, like Mary, collaborate with the collaborative God?

Mary as prophet. The world of the Bible is a man's world and the voice of women is often silenced. There are some exceptions in the Old Testament era – Deborah, Hannah, Judith, Esther – but they *are* the exceptions. The heroines of the Old Covenant are a strange group. Have a look, when you have a moment, at that extraordinary first chapter of Matthew's Gospel, that list of men who begat, all the generations from Abraham to Jesus. Much about the men, the begatters, not much about the women who laboured to bring each new son to birth. But in this fascinating genealogy, just occasionally a woman gets a mention – Tamar, involved in incest; Rahab the prostitute who helped the Israelites to capture Jericho; Ruth the outsider who came home with the widowed Naomi; Bathsheba seduced by King David; and Mary. It is an extraordinary list of marginalized women, and none of them till Mary has a voice. But then there is Mary, another marginalized woman, the one found pregnant before she and Joseph had come together, the one to be set aside, divorced, quietly. And suddenly Mary, in an ecstatic dialogue with her cousin Elizabeth, another woman despised and marginalized, for her barrenness, finds voice and sings the song, makes the protest and speaks the prophecy for the marginalized, the poor and the downtrodden. And it is a woman's voice. The prophets of old were Isaiah and Jeremiah, Micah and Hosea, Ezekiel and Malachi and more, but now, in that authentic tradition, the spokespeople of the Lord, comes Mary the prophet.

The danger, of course, is that you are so used to this protest song, Magnificat, that the Church sings every evening and has made safe with musical melodies, that you do not hear its radical message and its challenge. This is the song of feminine humanity and of downtrodden humanity that has found its voice:

He has looked with favour on the lowliness of his servant
Surely, from now on all generations will call me blessed:
for the Mighty One has done great things for me.
He has shown strength with his arm;
he has scattered the proud in the thoughts of their hearts.
He has brought down the powerful from their thrones,
and lifted up the lowly;
he has filled the hungry with good things,
and sent the rich away empty.

Here stands this pregnant woman, carrying a child, not pre-occupied with herself, but utterly engaged with God's justice, God's bias for the poor, God's judgement on the exploiters. She is the articulate herald of a new order, the one that her Son will bring into being.

Mary the prophet. And what about us? How the Church needs prophets today! People who listen to what God is try-ing to say to a deaf world and who find a voice to express it. Women and men, young and old, we need to see visions, dream dreams and articulate what God is saying to an alien-ated world, to a damaged Church, and to people for whom even the rumour of God's reality is being lost. We have become comfortable people. We have lost our radical cutting edge. We have ceased to be marginalized and dispossessed and we have lost the passion to speak for the marginalized and dispossessed. But God is for them. His Son lived among them. Mary was their prophet. You cannot hear her song, as in today's Gospel, let alone sing it in the liturgy, without being ready to look for the prophetic message in your own community or even to discover that it is going to be heard only when you find your voice.

Mary as god-bearer. In the Greek, the word is *theotokos*, the one who carries God. It is the ultimate description of Mary. Because she is full of grace, because of her role as collaborator, the Spirit works in her and she carried in her womb the one who is as much God as he is human, Jesus Christ. There's a lovely line in Elizabeth Jennings' poem, 'The Annunciation':

It is a human child she loves,
though a God stirs beneath her breast
and great salvations grip her side.

I don't want to say much about this profound title, just two things. First, simply that it is worth holding on to, using with thankful devotion when you think of Mary or see her portrayed in art. At the very heart of faith, she isn't what matters. She is simply a vessel, a vessel for the divine, the means by which God came uniquely among a people in a way that has changed everything. Because she was that vessel, all generations are to call her blessed, but she doesn't point to herself. She carries Christ into the world. That was how he was first among his people, hidden in the Virgin's womb.

That's the first thing about god-bearer. This is the other. It's like that again now. Christ's glory fills the universe, but he is not seen on earth as he was in the days of his incarnation. Yes, his glory fills the universe, but he is among his people, hidden, not in their wombs, but in their hearts and minds and bodies, and wherever they go they carry Christ into the dark places, the hurting places, and the unexpecting places of the world. In other words, for all the uniqueness of Mary as *theotokos*, you also are to be a god-bearer. You must, every day in every way, carry Christ into every place and every circumstance where his love and compassion and life are longed for. God-bearers are we all.

Mary the collaborator, Mary the prophet, Mary the god-bearer. Mary the sister. Of course we talk of Mary as mother and there is biblical support for that as the dying Lord looks down from the cross and entrusts Mary to the Beloved Disciple, who is seen as representing the Church, with the words 'Here is your mother'. Mother Mary is a strong and attractive image for many. But Mary, not as mother, but as sister?

The language of relationships in the Christian community is much more about brothers and sisters than about mothers and fathers. Mary as our sister conveys the truth that she is our companion in faith, a friend and an encourager, and something of a model, but not one on a pedestal. She is essentially and entirely human; crucially she is one of us. She is our sister.

She is. She is our sister in the communion of saints. Both sentences are important. Mary *is*, not Mary *was*. Mary *is*. And that is possible because of the communion of saints, that wonderful part of the divine providence that we should all belong together in a great company of those who praise and pray and make pilgrimage towards God, supporting one another, upholding one another, in a fellowship that has no hierarchy, but is held together by mutual honour and love. That's the Mary who is my sister and yours. That's the Mary who, as she walks with us on the pilgrimage, may – just by her presence in our company – gently remind us that we too are called to be collaborators and prophets and god-bearers if the good news of her Son and Saviour is to be heard afresh in this generation, a generation that, if it will stop to think, will certainly call her blessed.

Holy Cross

It's a great day because some among us are to be confirmed. Note that little phrase – 'to be confirmed'. Not a great day because they are to confirm, but to be confirmed. There's something important there. They are going to confirm something – their faith in God, their love for Jesus, their desire to share in the life of the Church and that's very good. But, in the end, they are not here to confirm, but to be confirmed. And the principal confirming today is done by God. It's his faith in them, his love for them, their place in the life of the Church that he is confirming. He is the confirming God always wanting to pour his gifts, his grace, upon his children. Today he confirms his faith in, he confirms his love for, he confirms the place of those to be confirmed in the life of the Church. What they confirm is good. What God confirms makes it a great day.

I hope that perhaps they will remember that their confirmation was on the Eve of Holy Cross Day, which is a rather special day that occurs in the life of the Church each September. It's a day to celebrate the cross of Jesus, to give thanks for it, and to see how it relates to our lives. And a little later in the service, just before I lay my hand on the head of each candidate and say 'Confirm, O Lord, your servant with your Holy Spirit', I shall make the sign of the cross on their forehead with the holy oil. The sign of the cross, made on them once again, as it was when they were baptized.

There are four things the Scriptures tell us that I think are rather important for all of us who want to follow Jesus, and tonight especially important for those being confirmed.

The first is the call of Jesus to 'take up the cross'. And it is important to hear that call first without the word that is sometimes added – 'daily' – though I will come back to that. Jesus has, in Mark's and Matthew's Gospels, two basic invitations that almost become imperatives. The first is overwhelming, but has no hint of suffering: 'Follow me' and they did, and we have done so too, and become his disciples. You who are being confirmed tonight are doing just that, following him. But then he issues a tougher invitation, reinforcing the first, 'Take up your cross and follow me'. And I think the way Mark and Matthew understand it the meaning is this: 'Follow me, but know it will mean suffering, it will mean persecution; there is a cost to discipleship.' And that is part of what the cross calls forth from us, a willingness to embrace a path of discipleship that is costly. It's almost impossible for you and me to know what that might mean for some. We do not live in a culture where being a Christian leads to persecution and even to martyrdom. Some of our young people in their schools may have to make a costly stand for their faith more than older people. We do well to pause for a moment to remember with thanksgiving those who in many parts of the world witness for Christ with such cost to their discipleship that 'taking up the cross' is hardly a metaphor, but very close to reality. There could be circumstances in which you and I might be called to that kind of costly discipleship. But more often we identify with that call by our prayers for others who face the time of trial, whether in Nigeria or in Tanzania or the Sudan or in India, in every place where being a Christian is a dangerous business. But even if our witness, our taking up of the cross, is going to be a more simple matter, today the candidates are responding to that tougher call of Jesus, not just 'Follow me', but 'Take up your cross and follow me.'

But then there is Luke; and Luke adds to the words of Jesus 'every day' – 'Take up your cross every day and follow me.'

Perhaps he was writing out of a world where persecution was not so real, where the time of trial did not threaten so clearly, and discipleship was not so obviously costly. So he adds his 'every day' which gives us a different dimension. It moves the focus from persecution for the faith to things that seem cross-like in our experience of life from day to day.

For even in a culture without persecution, there are experiences of suffering that are so overwhelming or painful that they are experienced as carrying a heavy cross through life – every day. It never leaves you, it is always a burden. It may be a kind of disability, it may be an element of personality disorder, it may be constant physical pain. And it's part of the ambivalence of life that God seems sometimes to ask people to carry a burden that feels like a cross, yet also invites them to lean on him, to allow him to bear the weight for them. We need to be very wary of expressions like 'we all have our crosses to bear', for that could be used about trifling irritations and inconveniences that don't deserve to be associated with the sufferings of Christ. But 'every day' implies a consciousness of the cross all the time, a way of living life that sees the cross in every situation. And of course that is what our baptismal commitment means, the baptism we remember today when we go to the font, the baptismal commitment working out our salvation in terms of Christ's pattern of dying and living every day, so that *everything*, not just the things that obviously relate either to faith or to the trials of life, comes under the scrutiny of the cross.

So, first, 'take up your cross', and second, and subtly different, 'Take up your cross every day'. Third, 'look out from the cross'. Scripture never specifically tells us to do that, but it is implicit in the call to be like Christ, to be conformed to his image and his pattern. In other words, we are called to see the world, to see the Church, to see our human brothers and sisters, as Christ sees them, and as he saw them when as on the cross he felt himself drawing the whole world to him. Our task is not just to try to get inside the mind of Peter or Pilate, the high priest or the centurion, or Mary who anointed his feet or

Mary who stood at the cross. It is to try to get into the mind of Christ, to experience, as far as our imagination will allow, what he experienced and so to be conformed to his way of breathing and living and dying. To look with love upon the world and with yearning for its peace and the wholeness of its peoples. So to look out from the cross is always part of our vocation, to try to be where Christ is, to see with his eyes and to love with his love. Jesus invites you to do that today, to look out on his world with his eyes and to love with his love and to commit yourselves to work for its peace and its healing.

But finally, 'gaze upon the cross'. Not carry it, nor even look down from it, but fix one's eyes upon it and wonder at the love it represents, wonder at the life it gives, wonder at the strange hidden glory that John believed was there. 'Now the Son of Man has been glorified and God has been glorified in him. If God has been glorified in him, God will also glorify him in himself and will glorify him at once.' And the glory for John shines forth from the cross. And to worship, to adore, to be silent and to be profoundly moved, is the only authentic response. One of the moments in the liturgy of Holy Week that touches me most deeply is to see people move through the church to kneel for a moment, or to stand if kneeling is too difficult, at the foot of the cross, to pray or perhaps just to wonder at the mysterious heart of faith that in this rough-hewn wood is hidden a tree of glory, of triumph, of life restored.

So, each one of you, on this Feast of the Holy Cross, and those of you on whom the cross will once again be marked today just before the Holy Spirit is called down upon you once more to give you strength to walk with Jesus:

- Take up the cross.
- Take up the cross every day.
- Look out from the cross.
- Gaze at the cross.

And, in doing all these, find yourself drawn to the Father, close to Jesus, and filled with the Holy Spirit.

The Feast of Bishop Lancelot Andrewes

Holy, holy, holy is the LORD of hosts; the whole earth is full of his glory. (Isa. 6.3)

Thus call the seraphim one to another in Isaiah's visionary experience in the temple wherein he both encounters the sheer holiness of God and hears the call to ministry. For those of you being admitted or licensed today, my prayer is that you are experiencing in this service at least a glimpse of that sense of the reality of God that must first have overwhelmed you for you even to consider offering yourself as a reader, and at least an echo in the words I put to you in this service of the call to ministry you then received. And my prayer goes further. It is that, all through your life, you will go on being swept off your feet by the wonder of the God to whom the seraphim acclaim 'Holy, holy, holy is the LORD of hosts', and will go on hearing the insistent invitation to be God's man or woman in a sinful world and will go on responding, 'Lord, send me.' All through your life and especially when you share in worship, whether leading it or simply participating with others in it. Don't ever grow used to it, the wonder of God and the marvel of his call to you. Never take them for granted. Praise him for them every day – the wonder of God and the marvel of his call.

If you do, you will be very like the man the Church celebrates today, Lancelot Andrewes, scholar, preacher, wordsmith, and much more, Bishop of Chichester and then of Winchester, who died on this day in 1626 and whose tomb you will find in Southwark Cathedral. There are three books concerning Andrewes that I took down off my shelves yesterday. One you would have difficulty getting hold of, F. E. Brightman's classic 1903 hardback translation of Andrewes's *Private Prayers*. The second is an excellent biography of him by Paul Welsby, published in 1964 and which a good library would provide for you. The third is a wonderful translation of the *Private Prayers*, selected and edited by David Scott. It is treasure and I commend it to you – a book to read and a book with which to pray. If you know nothing of Lancelot Andrewes, one of the great Anglicans of the seventeenth century, probably of all time, it's worth putting that right. It will be enormously enriching and rewarding. Today I can only tell you a very little.

But tell you I will, for his life and his writings have much to say, I believe, to the reader, to each one of you. There are five attributes – I mention each one just briefly.

First, Lancelot Andrewes was a man with time for the Scriptures. We know that because he devoted a significant part of his life, while Dean of Westminster, to work on what we now call the Authorized or King James version of the Bible. He chaired the group that worked on all the books from Genesis to Kings. We know it also because his book of *Private Prayers* is full of quotations from Scripture, crafted creatively into prayers, but words of Scripture none the less. But neither of these facts get to the heart of it. He was steeped in the Scriptures. They gave shape and pattern to his life. And that only comes from prayerful reading, careful study and disciplined reflection. Brothers and sisters, if you are to preach, you also must be steeped in the Scriptures. A quick glance at the readings for the Sunday is not enough. Daily opening of the Bible, regular study, possession of commentaries, exposure to the text, nothing less will do. Not that it should be an exacting task, but a joyful rewarding exploration. And when you are there in the pulpit, for all that your sermon may begin with a story, may include a bit of humour, certainly will relate to contemporary issues, make sure it engages with Scripture, wherein is God's word for this and for every generation. Serious preaching takes the Bible seriously. Lancelot Andrewes knew that.

Second – and you might think this was the same point, but I don't think it is – he was a man with a reverence for words. He was considered the outstanding preacher of his day and his sermons have withstood the test of time, for they were crafted with the patient skill of the wordsmith who has a concern for truth, for rhythm, for poetry, for memorability. Andrewes loved to pray the Scriptures in their original languages, whether Hebrew or Greek, though he preached of course in fine English in just the same way as he helped to create in the 1611 Bible a text of unparalleled beauty. T. S. Eliot thought Andrewes a superb writer and used a lot of Andrewes's texts as an inspiration for his poetry.

A cold coming they had of it, at this time of the year, just the worst time to take a journey, and specially a long journey ... the ways deep, the weather sharp, the days short, the sun farthest off ... the dead of winter.

Eliot's *Journey of the Magi*? No, Andrewes's words the inspiration for Eliot's poem.

Words matter, getting the words right matters. It matters because the words of worship, whether the prayers or the preaching, carry our doctrine. What we believe is formed by the words of the liturgy that we use over and over again and by the words of the sermon, especially if it is preached with flair and conviction. How important it is that the words we say reflect Christian truth. Of course there is a place for spontaneity, for the extempore, and of course God hears the prayer of the heart, however inarticulate or unpolished, but never must that be an excuse for words in worship that lack beauty or theological clarity. God must be given the best. And words matter because Christ is himself the Word of God, the logos. We speak of the

One who is the Word, the One whose very existence is a Word from the Father. Lancelot Andrewes was right to have a reverence for words. And you need that too. Your commission is not to chat about Jesus or to give a talk. It is to preach Christ, the Eternal Word of the Father, and that is an awesome ministry of words well chosen.

A man with time for the Scriptures, a man with a reverence for words and, third, a man with a priority for prayer. I've hinted at this already, for Andrewes is remembered above all else for his *Private Prayers*, published after his death, probably never intended to be public, which are sometimes highly developed complete texts and sometimes little more than notes and jottings, ideas and mentions, especially in intercession, arranged by days of the week. Listen to this from his provision for Saturday. First Intercession:

> *O heavenly King*
> *strengthen our faithful monarchs*
> *establish the faith*
> *calm the nations*
> *give peace to the world*
> *protect this holy place*
> *set the members of our family who have gone to their rest*
> *before us*
> *in the tabernacles of the just,*
> *and we who come to you in good faith and with true*
> *repentance,*
> *receive you,*
> *O good and gracious lover of your people.*

Or, more intimately

> *O Lord, supply*
> *to my faith, virtue,*
> *to my virtue, knowledge,*
> *to my knowledge, temperance,*
> *to my temperance, patience,*

to my patience, godliness,
to my godliness, charity,
to my charity, love
that I forget not that I was forgiven my former sins,
but may have diligence to make my calling, and my election,
    sure, through good works.

Or this little gem of a prayer:

Strength of the Father, shepherd me.
Wisdom of the Son, enlighten me.
Power of the Spirit, quicken me.

Here is a man with a priority for prayer. It is not just that he spent five hours a day in prayer, but that he had given time to ordering his prayer life. The *Private Prayers* are essentially his weekly planned cycle of prayer. There is a connection between this and his power as a preacher. Because he turned aside to be with God so often, there was much of God he could proclaim. Because he knew God and loved him intimately, there was so much to share. If ever you find you are due to preach and you have nothing to say, return with all your heart to prayer. Those who drink deeply have the living water to share. We've rather given up the old discipline whereby the preacher fell to his knees during the hymn before the sermon to seek divine help for the preaching he was about to do. Perhaps that is a pity, for it was a kind of symbolic reminder that sermons come out of time on our knees as much as out of time in front of our computer. Brothers and sisters, go on giving priority to prayer.

But then, rather differently, I need to say that Lancelot Andrewes was a man engaged with the world. Man of Scripture, man of words, man of prayer, yes, but living out his life at court, the court of James I, many of his sermons preached before a royal audience, many of them engaging with issues of the day, and a bishop, involved with the life of his diocese. This is no hermit figure with whom we are dealing, but a man in touch with the real world and preaching tellingly into it.

Dean of Westminster – we know what the Westminster world is like. In other words, Lancelot Andrewes took seriously the calling to make connections. Soaked in the Scriptures, a reverent wordsmith, a man of prayer, he made connections between the life of faith and the truth of the gospel on the one hand, and the realities of the contemporary world on the other. And that's your task too. Always make connections. Always relate. The good news does not inhabit a private sealed or bubble-wrapped world. It throws shafts of light on the issues of the day if only you would make connections.

But I want to end by making explicit what has been implicit up to now, not least in the choice for the first reading on Lancelot Andrewes's Day of that powerful passage from Isaiah 6. Ultimately what matters is that Andrewes was a man with a sense of God. He could create the wonderful prose of the King James Bible because the words came alive for him, for they spoke of the activity of a living God whom he knew and loved. His prayers are so authentic because they are the prayers of the heart to one in whom he put his trust with his whole being, heart and soul and mind and strength. His sermons communicated the goodness of God in a fallen world because experience had taught him that God was alive and active in that world for all its sin and folly. Yes, he had a sense of God. And so must you, which is why, like him, you must keep coming back to the sense of the reality of God that must first have overwhelmed you and to the echo of the call to ministry when you first received it. And you must seek the renewal of that sense and that echo for every day and month and year that you are a reader and a Christian in God's world.

Take Lancelot Andrewes as a model. Be men and women with time for the Scriptures, with reverence for words, with priority for prayer, with engagement with the world, with a sense of God.

Holy, holy, holy is the LORD *of hosts; the whole earth is full of his glory.* (Isa. 6.3)

Behaving, Believing, Belonging

This is a wonderful celebration and I'm glad we are all sharing in it, candidates, families, friends, people who are often in church and familiar with our ways, perhaps some others less familiar. Everyone is welcome. Everyone is welcome to be drawn into the three really important things we are going to do.

First, gathering around the font (or turning towards it) we are going to renew the covenant made at our baptism. It is when we are baptized that we celebrate God's gift of life, claim his blessing, express our desire to belong to Jesus Christ and to his Church, begin a journey of faith. And God responds to all that – indeed, he is already bringing that about – even before we have asked. It is a celebration of our entry into Christian discipleship and today all of us willing to do so and, particularly those who today are to be confirmed, grasp the opportunity to reaffirm all that happened in our baptism – in some cases, long ago – and the water is sprinkled over us to help us remember what God did when we were baptized.

Second, there is confirmation. It is a kind of extension of baptism. People come to it at different stages in their life, some when they are still quite young, some when they are really quite old. There isn't a right age, though there is a right time for each person. And in confirmation, with the anointing with the holy oil, the laying of the bishop's hand on the head and the prayers of the whole community, God confirms everything he has promised in baptism and, crucially, the abiding presence of the Holy Spirit.

And third there is Holy Communion, the Eucharist. It is something the Church celebrates every week, which could mean you took it for granted. But you should never do that. It is one of God's wonderful gifts. We do what Jesus invited, commanded, us to do. Just like at the supper the night before he died, just like the meal on the evening of the day he rose again, we take the bread, give thanks, break and share. We take a cup of wine also and share that too. For some today this may be their first sharing in Holy Communion and that's a very special moment. But sharing in Holy Communion is not meant to have rarity value. The invitation to come and eat is one Jesus issues to us week in week out and it goes on being special, even the five hundredth time and beyond.

Three things, the Church calls them sacraments – baptism, confirmation, Eucharist – and each of them a delight, all of them together a wonderful experience of God's presence in our lives.

Mixed in with all of that, there are three sets of questions today to those being confirmed. You might say they are about behaving, believing and belonging. Let me take each in turn very briefly.

There are the behaving questions. They are about the kind of lives we want to lead. They begin with some negatives because there are always some things we want to leave behind, so we can start again, the new life of the Christian. Do you reject, renounce, repent – leave behind the things that drag you down, the things that separate you from God, the things of which you feel guilty or ashamed? It is right to start there, but not to stop there, so the questions move on immediately and jump from the negative to the positive. Do you turn to Christ, submit to Christ, come to Christ? And that's because God's invitation is always to be positive about life, to enjoy life, and to live a fulfilled life, and the key to that is to allow your life to be shaped by a relationship with Jesus Christ and to model your behaviour on his life of love. So there is today an invitation to adopt a lifestyle that follows Jesus, to be a disciple, to allow your behaviour to follow a pattern that he will give you.

That's behaving. Then there is believing. We are invited to make our own the faith of the Church, expressed in the words of the Apostles' Creed, affirming our belief in God, as Father, Son and Holy Spirit. Part of that belief, of course, is our faith in what Jesus has done for us, in his dying on the cross, which brings forgiveness of our sins and mends our relationship with God. And we can be particularly thankful for that in relation to those other questions about behaving, because however much we try to live good and moral lives, we know we mess up sometimes, the behaving all goes to pieces. But our believing assures us that God has sorted that through Jesus on the cross. And, in the end, Christianity is more about believing than behaving, putting our trust in God, believing that God believes in you and me, loves us, embraces us, enfolds us, nourishes us. Yes, I believe in a God who believes in me.

Sometimes, of course, our faith is strong, confident, full of energy and joy. I hope it is like that for many of you being confirmed today. For most people it can't be like that all of the time. Sometimes our faith is weak, confused, fragile. Sometimes we can even lose it for a while, though I don't believe God ever loses his faith in you and me. Sometimes we just have to stick on in there with as much faith as we can muster. And God honours that. God's invitation is always to put our trust in him, to love him, and to allow ourselves to be drawn towards him, but God gives us space to explore our believing. He draws us to himself with patience and gentleness.

Behaving, believing, belonging. There is one more set of questions I shall put to us all today. The service calls these questions the Commission. They are about joining in with the Church and about playing our part in God's world. Will you continue, I ask of us all, in the teaching and the fellowship and the Eucharist and the prayers? Will you seek and serve Christ, loving your neighbour as yourself? Will you pray for the world, defend the weak, seek peace and justice? These are questions about recognizing that you do not live in isolation. You belong, belong in your church, belong in your community, belong in our society, belong to God's world, and that belonging brings responsibility. Today you can rejoice that you belong, you are never alone, but then you need to commit yourselves to living with the responsibilities that belonging brings.

Behaving, believing, belonging. All three are important. They don't always, of course, neatly come like that as three distinct elements of our lives. They are all mixed in together and people experience them very differently. Some people find belonging first. They can belong to the Church for a long time before they can say with real conviction that they believe. That's all right with God. Belonging is often where you need to be before you can begin to sort of believe. And belonging is often where you need to be even when you haven't yet got the behaving right. God copes with that, but what God wants for you, not so much from you as for you, is that through your Christian pilgrim-age – a lifetime of journeying with Jesus – you will come to walk the Jesus way (behaving), to have faith in God who loves you unconditionally (believing), and to play your part in God's mission (belonging to Christ's Church and working for God's kingdom on earth).

Now all that promising about behaving, believing and belonging might make you think that what is going on today is that you are doing the confirming that gives this service its name – confirmation. But, important as what you are doing is, you'd be wrong. For the one who is doing the most important confirming isn't you, but God. God confirms today. That, in the end, is why this is a wonderful day.

Let me tell you what God confirms. First, God confirms his grace. We'll pray later, 'Defend, O Lord, these your servants with your heavenly grace'. And grace is what God pours upon us to enrich our lives irrespective of what we deserve – love, protection, friendship, blessing, and all of it through our rela-tionship with God's Son Jesus Christ. It is through Jesus that we experience the love, the protection, the friendship, the bless-ing of God. And that's grace and it is a free gift of a generous

God. And today God is confirming that gift, given in baptism, for each one of you being confirmed.

Second, God confirms the presence within you of his Holy Spirit, the Spirit, who is part of God himself, living within you, animating you, energizing you, sharing God's love with you in such a way that there is enough love for you to share with those around you. The Spirit lives within you, 'abides' within you as Jesus puts it, but also comes with particular intensity at key moments in your life, just as the Spirit came upon Mary at the annunciation and Jesus at his baptism and on the disciples at Pentecost. And today we pray that God will confirm you with his Holy Spirit as you come to confirmation, so there is a leap forward in your relationship with God and your understanding of what God wants for you and for your life as a disciple of Jesus Christ.

God gives you his grace. God gives you the Holy Spirit. God gives you the bread of life. Jesus himself is, of course, the bread of life, and his chosen way of feeding you, nourishing you, making you strong and fit and healthy for the living of your life, is to give you in the Eucharist the bread that becomes for us his body and the wine that becomes for us his blood. That's a way of saying that he gives you a share in his life, his risen life, his eternal life, that is life indeed. And this gift of the bread of life God confirms not only today, but every time you come. Every time you stretch out your hand and receive the bread, simple unsophisticated gift as it seems, Jesus is offering you a share in his life. That's something to treasure more and more as the years go by.

That's why today what really matters is what God confirms. God gives you his grace, God gives you the Holy Spirit. God gives you the bread of life. The grace, the Spirit, the bread.

Michaelmas

'Michael and his angels fought against the dragon; the dragon and his angels fought back, but they were defeated.' It might be no surprise to you that I like that verse of Scripture, a Michael on the side of right who prevails! The Scriptures assert the existence of a prince of the heavenly host, Michael the archangel. You can meet him five times in Scripture, three times in the Book of Daniel, once in the somewhat obscure Epistle of Jude and, by name, just this once in the Book of Revelation. His name, of course, means 'Who is like God', which is a good name to have, but a rather steep challenge. I love the poetry of that passage from Revelation with the defeat of evil. But in some ways it is a rather depressing passage, worrying even, for the heavens are to rejoice, because the devil has been banished, sent to exile, so that heaven is a place of pure good and beauty. But woe to the earth, the place of exile, because that is where the evil one has taken up residence now.

Evil does not live in heaven. It lives on earth. And in a way we don't need Scripture to tell us that. We know it for ourselves. We see things on television and we read in the newspapers that dreadful despicable things happen on the earth, that greed and violence and lust and abuse all occupy the earth. The devil has indeed come down to us with great wrath, to use the biblical imagery. Evil flourishes. And, in our more honest moments, we also know that evil is not simply around us, but within us. Each one of us is a complex mix of good and bad, selfishness and selflessness, and we don't expect to see that entirely sorted out in this life; we are victims of what the Bible calls the fall.

But the Christian faith is always *good* news. So what is this good news at Michaelmas as we celebrate St Michael and All Angels? Well the angels are themselves the first part of the good news. There is a kind of arrogance in thinking, as some do, that angels are make-believe. Only arrogant humans could believe they were the only beings God could create. Today's collect affirms that God created us, yes, mortals, but also that he created angels. And we have heard about the angels and the ladder. It's a striking and attractive picture – a ladder between earth and heaven and the angels ascending and descending, keeping the two connected.

The Scriptures present us with two predominant activities of angels, one towards God, one towards us. Towards God they offer praise, adoration and worship. They are pictured constantly around the throne of God, held by God's holiness and his beauty, wrapped in attention to him, singing God's praise. And that is in itself a source of encouragement to you and me. It means that, when we worship God, when we are seeking to be drawn into that experience of communion with heaven, there are others already fully engaged; we are simply clocking in to their ceaseless activity. And, when our own attempts are fairly feeble (and that has been known!), then there's encouragement also in the fact that their prayers and praises are confident, constant and strong.

But the picture of the angels (and, of course, it is just picture language, but it clothes a deep reality that it is impossible to express except in pictures) is one both of constant worship in heaven, but also of dancing up and down the ladder, the ladder that touches the ground. It is as if, deserting the gathering around the throne for a while, each in their turn, the angels slip down the ladder and touch the ground and maybe take us back up the ladder with them or, if not our whole selves, at least our hopes, our longings and our prayers. They sweep them up as they touch the ground so that they, we, although we live on the earth where evil has its hold, are transported, albeit fleetingly, into that place from which evil has been banished and all is pure, all is good, all is lovely. And we need to be transported there sometimes to renew our confidence in God, in goodness, in beauty, lest the ugliness of some of the things in this world might oppress us or disillusion us.

So picture the angels around the throne. Picture the angels dancing up and down the ladder. Picture your hopes, your longings and your prayers ascending.

Now think for a moment about Jacob who dreams and sees the angels ascending and descending.

And when he wakes up he says:

Surely the Lord *is in this place – and I did not know it! ... How awesome is this place! This is none other than the house of God, and this is the gate of heaven.* (Gen. 28.16–17)

And he's not in church; this is in the open air, an ordinary place where he has lain down to sleep, but he senses that God is present, inhabiting the space. The angels have disappeared, but God is inhabiting the space. This is the house of God, the gate of heaven. And that's really important, isn't it? It's a hint that not only do the angels take our hopes, our prayers and our longings up the ladder as they keep their angelic movement going, but as they descend they bring with them a little bit of heaven that they drop on the earth, a little bit of God that takes root on the earth, so that, although our eyes and our minds are drawn to heaven, that is not the only place where we may sense the presence of God. He is in our midst. He is present in our beautiful, yet ugly, complex world. Heaven on earth, God with us.

And that brings me to the other function the Scriptures assign to angels. They are messengers. Indeed, that is literally what their name means. They enable the word of God to be heard. The Bible is full of the stories of the angels bringing God's word to those to whom he would speak, never more beautifully than when that other archangel, Gabriel, unfolded to Mary the divine intention that she should be the mother of his Son. In the angel, God's voice is heard. In the angel, God all but becomes visible for a moment.

So the function of the ascending and descending angels is to enable us to hear the voice of God. It is always a voice of re-assurance, of welcome, of affirmation, of love. That's the kind of God that God is. We may live in a world marred by evil, but we are the friends of a God who pours his grace upon us to help us see the beauty beyond the ugliness, to sense his abiding presence, to equip us for the task of standing with him for goodness, righteousness and peace. The two-way communi-cation between earth and heaven ensures that.

But here we have to look at John's Gospel, for you have to compare what the two readings say about the ladder and the holy ones who ascend and descend. Listen again.

And he dreamed that there was a ladder set up on the earth, the top of it reaching to heaven; and the angels of God were ascending and descending on it. (Gen. 28.12)

And this is John:

[Jesus said] 'Very truly, I tell you, you will see heaven opened and the angels of God ascending and descending upon the Son of Man.' (John 1.51)

You can picture the ladders and the angels, but do you see where the focus is in John? It is on Jesus. In a way Jesus has become the ladder. The angels are ascending and descending upon him. Jesus has become the link between earth and heaven. The angels, for all the beauty of their dance, are less important that the one who makes it possible for them to come and go, to ascend and descend. The early Christians sometimes referred to Jesus as 'God's angel'. He is, of course, not so much God's voice as God's word. And the angels themselves, of course, as we know from the Christmas story as they hovered over the fields where there were shepherds keeping watch over their flocks, brought in their ultimate message that God was no longer speaking through their voices, but through a Son, a Son who would not come down a ladder and go up again straight away after a brief glance over the earth, but would live among us, live, die, save, rise again and only then return, and even then with a promise to be with us till the end of time. Michael may have sent the dragon down to the earth, but God sent his Son down to the earth so that ultimately that dragon should not prevail, evil should not have the last word. The cross would fix that.

So the Feast of St Michael and All Angels calls us to recognize the reality of evil, but to rejoice in the angels and the ladder that joins earth to heaven, ensuring that we can join in the worship offered there and receive the grace that comes from there and, above all, honour Christ who is the Ladder, overcoming evil, leading us to God.

Harvest Thanksgiving

There's a choice for a preacher at a harvest service about the kind of line to take. At one level it is all very simple. The church building at harvest is itself a kind of sermon, filled with the fruits of the earth and all the things that sustain our daily life. Just look at it and rejoice, give thanks. Do we need a sermon? But, of course, there are some very deep issues that do perhaps need bringing to the surface.

One is about how the fruits of the earth come to be, how the wind and the rain and the sunshine that allow the harvest to come to fruition come to be. Is it a matter of chance? Or can it all be explained by scientific laws? Or is there still a need to recognize behind it all the hand of a creator God. That, despite the onslaught of Stephen Hawking and Richard Dawkins, is what people of faith continue to believe. It is an understanding that has intellectual weight and it needs to be restated with confidence and energy in the face of a secularizing anti-religious agenda. Harvest can be the right time for that sort of sermon as we celebrate the creator God who brought this intricate, beautiful and mysterious world into being. I believe passionately in that amazing God.

Or there is another sermon about justice, peace, the integrity of creation and God's bias for the poor. We live in a world where the Creator has given sufficient for everyone to be fed, for none to go hungry, for all to be satisfied. We ought to be able to give thanks today for a world of plenty equitably shared. Instead we live in a world where some have too much, obscenely too much, and others do not have sufficient to live a healthy life or to flourish into old age. And the obscenely too much is being exploited in such a way that not only produces world poverty in our own day, but also condemns future generations as we use extravagantly and selfishly the resources that ought to be conserved for future generations. And that, Christians believe, is not only foolish and certainly unethical, but deeply offends the justice of God and deeply wounds the God who made the world, saw that it was good, ensured there was plenty, and desires life in abundance for all God's children. And, if there are communities that think too narrowly about the harvest, focusing just on what they can see around them and on the fact that their own bellies are full, then they need to hear a harvest sermon that makes them feel uncomfortable about the narrowness of their worldview. I believe passionately in that God of justice.

But this morning I want to do something much more simply – but, I think, equally important. I want to create a prayer, a short simple memorable prayer, that you might pray not just today, but many times over. It has just ten words to it – first two, then three, then two more and then a final three. All ten words come to me as I look at the story we have just heard of the feeding of the great multitude by Jesus. As a matter of fact the prayer, for all its simplicity, keeps us in mind of the great themes, of the place of God in creation and of the kind of world of plenty God desires for all his sons and daughters.

Here are the first two words – 'Generous God'. We need, right at the start of our prayer, to know to whom we are speaking. People find all sorts of adjectives to describe the God who, at one and the same time, is both wrapped in mystery yet revealed to us by Jesus Christ. 'Almighty' is one of them – there is nothing beyond God's power. 'Eternal' is another – there is no time outside God's reach. But rather more of our prayers, I think, ought to begin 'Generous God'. It is in God's very nature always to be giving and the gifts God gives are life-giving. The creation is itself a generous gift, God's desire to share, to create a place where people might experience the joy and the love, the richness and the life, within his being and his heart. Each individual life, yours and mine, is a gift of a generous God who makes us in his own image; in other words, to be like him, feeling as he feels, loving as he loves, longing as he longs. A crucial part of his generosity is that it is poured out freely whether we deserve it or not. It is unmerited. It is simply the way God is. He pours out his generous life-giving love and that we call 'grace'. And the grace comes with such extravagance that there is more than we need and lots left over so we can pass some of it on in lives that reflect that divine generosity. The grace did – does, of course – reach its high point in God's greatest gift, the gift of his Son, in Jesus, who embodied the generosity of God supremely when he gave (note the word 'gave') his life for his friends.

And here in this story we see the generous God at work in this Jesus who embodies his generosity. For Jesus takes the simple provisions that the boy has brought, the bread and the fish, and he makes from it sufficient for all the hungry people to be fed and, furthermore, for there to be much left over, twelve baskets full no less. Quite how it all happened nobody can quite explain. Some people think that Jesus created such an atmosphere of generosity that all sorts of people dug around in their bags and found sufficient food not only to feed themselves, but the neighbours around them who hadn't brought anything – not realizing how long they would be away from home and how far from the shops. That in itself would have been the work of a generous God. But that is really to miss the point. The point is not that Jesus brought out the generosity of the crowd, though praise the Lord if he did, but that God provided, the generous God provided, sufficient and more than sufficient, because that is the kind of God he is, always meeting poverty with riches, always providing for the poor.

So that's how our simple ten-word prayer needs to begin – 'Generous God'.

And then come three key words – 'we thank you'. That too

comes out of our story. For at the heart of it is Jesus giving thanks. Giving thanks is his characteristic thing. In story after story in the Gospels, just like here, Jesus takes bread into his hands – and in this story fish, in others it might be wine – and gives thanks, blesses, 'says grace' we might say. And I'm always keen people should know that the proper name for what we are celebrating today is 'Harvest Thanksgiving', rather than 'Harvest Festival'. Christians are always meant to be thankful people, with thankfulness deep in their hearts, and more often than not also on their lips. It's thankfulness first of all for the people we take for granted – and there are many of those at harvest time, all the people involved in food production and distribution; thankfulness for the farmers certainly, but they are only the beginning of a wonderful chain of people ensuring we have food and drink when we want it. And thankfulness for the harvest itself, the gracious gift of God, thankfulness for Jesus who shows us the character of God and models for us the life of thankfulness, Jesus of a joyful bubbling prayer, 'Father, I thank you ...' Thankfulness for all this to God the giver. That's the second part of the prayer – 'we thank you'. We are halfway there now, five of our ten words, 'Generous God, we thank you.'

And here are the next two words, 'for bread'. All the meal stories in the Gospels speak of bread. Sometimes just bread, sometimes bread and wine, sometimes bread and fish, but always bread. And for Jesus, of course, bread was part of his message; indeed, so much so that he spoke of himself 'as the bread of life', 'the bread come down from heaven'. Bread is the staple food that satisfies; not a luxury, but a simple necessity. 'Give us today our daily bread', we pray and, though you can spiritualize that, making it apply to our religious needs, its most straightforward interpretation is probably the wisest. God wants to give us the food that makes our bodies nourished and healthy. So, though we may be thankful for exotic foods, for rich fare and for the amazing variety you find on the menu when you eat out, or look at longingly in the supermarket, your wisest gratitude is for bread, the food that the rich and the poor alike need to have, the staple food that keeps us alive, the loaves with which Jesus fed the multitude in the desert, the simple food that brings to mind the way Jesus took bread into his hands as he looked up to heaven to the Father and said the blessing. Give thanks for the simple things. Never take them for granted. Never undervalue them. Maybe resolve to stick rather more with them in solidarity with the poor. Think of those for whom bread is a luxury. Think of those who do not always have their daily bread. 'Generous God, we thank you for bread.'

And here are the last words to complete the prayer – 'to share together'. There's a lot of working together in that story, people together, teamwork, sharing. Andrew working with the lad with the loaves and fishes, Jesus working with him too, and then the disciples getting everyone organized, sat down and fed, a massive distribution of food. And, of course, behind all that was God in collaboration with Jesus, with the disciples, with the boy. Do you know the origin of that lovely word 'companion'? 'Companion' literally means 'one with whom you share bread'. Sharing bread creates friendship. Gathering around a table to eat together makes relationship. Eating on your own is no fun; you can never call it a feast. Sharing makes all the difference. And it is in sharing together that you can change things. Together, collaborating, you can feed the hungry, make better communities, maintain the life of the town, make the Church grow. Sharing, working together, can change lives. So our prayer is never for sufficient bread for ourselves, but always for sufficient bread for sharing. 'Generous God, we thank you for bread to share together.'

It is a very simple prayer, but I think it is a profound one, for it celebrates the kind of God we believe in, reminds us that thankfulness should be at the heart of our lives, brings us back to simplicity, and invites us to share. A good message, a good prayer, for harvest. Why don't you memorize it and pray it often, for there are important truths hidden within it. And, not least because you learn something better by saying it out loud, let's pray it now together, slowly first in its four parts:

Generous God – we thank you – for bread – to share together.
And again:
Generous God – we thank you – for bread – to share together.

The Last Sunday after Trinity, Bible Sunday, Year B

We have arrived at one of those turning points in the Christian year. On Wednesday it will be All Saints' Day and our focus through November will be on the kingdom of Christ, the fellowship of the saints, and the life of heaven. And that will bring us, in the Christian cycle, to Advent. But today is the last of the Sundays after Trinity, the summer weeks of green. The collect that we have already prayed is a rather striking one. In the old Prayer Book it belongs in Advent, but now we use it today, the Last Sunday after Trinity.

> *Blessed Lord, who caused all holy scriptures to be written for our learning:*
> *help us so to hear them, to read, mark, learn and inwardly digest them.*

It's a beautiful piece of writing and a memorable prayer and, of course, it invites us to reflect on what the Scriptures mean for us, what part the Bible plays in our lives. Just as a fascinating aside, the scholars believe the original ran slightly differently. Not 'so to hear them, to read, mark, learn', but 'so to hear them read, mark, learn'. And that, of course, reflects an earlier culture where people were illiterate. They did not read, they 'heard read'. And hearing the Scriptures read, which is what we do in the liturgy each Sunday, is part of that and is something that needs to be done with care and clarity and passion. I'm rather against the way we often bury our heads in a book or follow the reading on a sheet of paper. We ought, more often than not, to be all eyes on the reader and all ears for the words we hear persuasively proclaimed. That's 'hear them read'. But, yes, read, mark, learn and inwardly digest as well.

Our readings today take up the Bible theme and help to make this Bible Sunday. It's a day to remember and pray for those who make the Bible available and intelligible in our contemporary world: the biblical scholars and the theologians, the translators of the Scriptures, those who distribute them, the societies – the British and Foreign Bible Society, the Bible Reading Fellowship, Scripture Union, the Society for the Promoting of Christian Knowledge (SPCK). Yes, to remember and pray for all these.

But, chiefly, a day to help us to reflect on the place of the Bible in our lives and discipleship and, drawing on our readings, and especially on what Paul writes to Timothy, I want to put four imperatives before you this morning/evening. They are:

- Know the Scriptures.
- Use the Bible.
- Proclaim the message.
- Encounter the Word.

First, know the Scriptures. Paul writes to Timothy:

> *Continue in what you have learned and firmly believed, knowing from whom you learned it, and how from childhood you have known the sacred writings ...* (2 Tim. 3.14–15)

Timothy had grown up in a religious household, familiar with the Hebrew scriptures, so Paul can write to him in that manner. Many of us here also grew up with the Bible, the Hebrew scriptures we call the Old Testament, but the Christian Scriptures, which we call the New Testament, also. Some of us are of a generation where the Bible stories featured prominently in our schooling. Some of us remember fine biblical series on television

– *Jesus of Nazareth, Paul of Tarsus.* Some of us were taught to read the Bible every day. But, of course, not every one of us has that background. Some will remember that the only thing the Bible at home did was to sit unopened gathering dust. Some, more recently, will have grown up in a home where there was no Bible at all. Some will have gone through their education without encountering the Scriptures much. Not all of us can say how from childhood we have known the sacred writings.

But I hope we can all say that, whether long, long ago, or just recently, we have discovered what a treasure the Scriptures are and that we have resolved to know them better. Yes, to read, to mark, to learn, to inwardly digest, knowing that reflecting on them we can learn of the ways of God, of the story of Jesus, of the call to discipleship and of the meaning of life. Little of that is handed to you, as on a plate, in the Bible. Nearly all of it requires the kind of effort, engagement, struggle that 'read, mark, learn and inwardly digest' implies. But all that – the ways of God, the story of Jesus, the call to discipleship, the meaning of life – lies hidden there for those who will recognize the treasure and start digging.

I cannot imagine a Muslim who does not know the Koran. But I do know a lot of Christians who hardly know their Bibles. Their only encounter with the Scriptures is the public reading of them in church on Sunday. And in a world where people mock our faith, dismiss our faith, misunderstand our faith, that simply will not do. If you are a daily reader of the Bible, good for you. Keep at it. If you are not, this might be the day to make a resolution. Start with one of the Gospels. Start with just a few verses a day. Read, mark, learn and inwardly digest. Or, in the words of my imperative, seek to know the Scriptures.

Second, use the Bible. Paul writes to Timothy:

All scripture is inspired by God and is useful for teaching, for reproof, for correction, and for training in righteousness, so that everyone who belongs to God may be proficient, equipped for every good work. (2 Tim. 3.16–17)

Scripture is useful, Paul is saying, so use. It equips you.

We need to be honest. Using the Bible is not always easy. It doesn't simply tell you what to do. It's not one of those handbooks that save you puzzling things out and lead you straightforwardly to the solution of every problem. And sometimes, when it does seem to have some fairly straightforward instruction, you find either that somewhere else in the Scriptures it seems to be contradicted, or that the precise text seems at odds with the more general thrust of the Scriptures. The 200th anniversary of the bill to abolish slavery was in 2007. And that is an interesting case study, because those who fought to maintain slavery could point to many passages in the Bible that seemed to justify it quite emphatically. But the opponents of slavery had actually sensed the overall thrust of the Scriptures in terms of human dignity and freedom. Making sense of the Bible in that dispute was a challenge.

And, of course, it is the same today. Most of the issues that divide Christians turn out to be about the way we use the Bible. Women bishops and attitudes to homosexuality are both examples of where particular verses of Scripture seem at odds with the general tenor of the Bible, and the Church has to struggle to discern the word God has for us in the Scriptures in our generation.

But it is not only that we have to engage in something of a struggle as an institution. Each of us as an individual in relation to our belief and our core values and our ethical judgements needs to engage with the Bible, to use it, knowing that, although very few of the precise questions we are asking, let alone the answers we are seeking, are there for all to see (there in such a way you can't miss them), nevertheless the Church has found through reverent study through the centuries that God does speak to us through our use of the Scriptures; that they are, as Paul says, inspired by God. He speaks through them. They are for using and, if used, equip us. That's what Paul says. They equip us for every good work. They provide us with tools for daily life. So there is the second imperative: use the Bible. Don't just know what it says, though that's a start, but use it. Put it into action.

And third, proclaim the message. Paul puts it to Timothy in two ways. He says it in exactly that way:

> In the presence of God and of Christ Jesus, who is to judge the living and the dead ... I solemnly urge you: proclaim the message; be persistent whether the time is favourable or unfavourable; convince, rebuke, and encourage, with the utmost patience in teaching. (2 Tim. 4.1–2)

I hear that as a very clear message to me as a bishop. It could almost be my mission statement – to proclaim the message, to convince, to rebuke, to encourage, with the utmost patience in teaching. But I don't think he is talking to Timothy as a bishop, but simply as a Christian.

And then the same imperative comes again in slightly different words:

> As for you, always be sober, endure suffering, do the work of an evangelist ... (2 Tim. 4.5)

Proclaim the message. Do the work of an evangelist. And an evangelist is someone entrusted with the *evangel*, the same word as *gospel*. Proclaim the message. Talk about the gospel. Witness to the faith that is in you. That which we know from the Scriptures, that which we use in our lives from the Bible, we need to share with others. We are not good at it.

But the testimony to Jesus and to his works of love and power today will not be given unless you and I bear witness, proclaim the message. The world will not be offered the good news that it needs, if it is not to be lost, unless you and I do the work of evangelists. Finding your voice to speak of the faith that is in you, finding your voice to speak into the controversies of our world, finding your voice to be firm in the defence of truth and justice, this is what is required of you. Christians have an extraordinary ability to keep their faith to themselves.

It motivates them, inspires them, comforts them, shapes their lives, but somehow can still remain the secret they share only with God. We need a no-secret society culture in the Church, where we tell, where we witness, where we gossip the gospel for all its worth. The Scriptures are for sharing. If they can teach you and me of the ways of God, of the story of Jesus, of the call to discipleship and of the meaning of life, they can do it also for our society. But only if we proclaim the message. By your baptism into Jesus Christ, that task – duty, but joy – was laid upon you. It is not an optional part of discipleship. The Bible is not a secret handbook for those initiated into the Christian Church. It is a message for the world. That's the third imperative: proclaim the message. And there is an urgency about it.

Know the Scriptures. Use the Bible. Proclaim the message. Finally – encounter the Word. And you may think I've talked about that already. And, yes, I have talked about engaging with the words of the Scriptures. But John has a more subtle, and ultimately more fundamental, message. He is hinting at it in the word of Jesus:

You search the scriptures because you think that in them you have eternal life; and it is they that testify on my behalf. (John 5.39)

But it is right at the very beginning of his Gospel that John delivers his key message. 'In the beginning was the Word' and, a little later, 'The Word was made flesh and lived among us'. Ultimately, the Word of God for us is not a series of letters on a page or a parchment. The Word of God for us – Word, capital W, upper case – is Jesus Christ. There is a relation to the Scriptures, of course. It is in their pages that we meet this Jesus and learn his life-saving story. It is in their pages we learn how God prepared the way for his coming into the world. It is in their pages that we discover how the good news of Jesus soon turned into the life of the Church, his body. Without the words of the Scriptures, we would have no knowledge of Jesus

Christ. As Jesus says, the Scriptures testify to him. But, where we encounter the Word most profoundly is not in a book, however sacred, but in a person, in a relationship, in the one whom Scripture says is himself God's very Word to us. Everything that God wants us to mark, to learn, to inwardly digest, comes through our relationship with Jesus his Son, who by his very existence speaks to us more deeply of God than any words written down or handed on.

We struggle sometimes, when we hear the Bible read, with some of its more obscure passages, some of its more violent passages, some of its more counter-cultural passages, to say 'This is the word of the Lord'. We sometimes have our doubts. Discerning the word becomes a puzzle and a challenge. But, wonderfully, the Word we are most asked to receive is not a book of scriptures, but the Living One, the Living Word, to which those scriptures bear witness. And he, the one who came to live among us, the one who models for us goodness and humility and sacrifice and love, the one who died and rose again for us, is the one we encounter here week by week as we explore the word and share the sacrament. He is the one we meet in the Scriptures and in the bread and the wine over which we have given thanks. Praise the Lord for that and keep coming, so that the encounter can continue and the Word be more deeply planted in your hearts. The fourth imperative: encounter the Word.

Four imperatives for Bible Sunday:

- Know the Scriptures.
- Use the Bible.
- Proclaim the message.
- Encounter the Word.

No, four imperatives for *every* day:

- Know the Scriptures.
- Use the Bible.
- Proclaim the message.
- Encounter the Word.

All Saints Day

'Rejoice, people of God, and praise the Lord, keeping a holy day in honour of all God's saints.' That's how the old liturgies began for this feast we are keeping today, All Saints' Day. And rejoicing is certainly what we ought to do, for the communion of saints is a wonderful part of the providence of God. And I certainly rejoice to be celebrating it here with you, my presence a witness to our diocesan partnership, itself just a little part in that communion of saints.

So I bring you first the greetings of the people of the diocese of Gloucester, of the cathedral just next to where I live, and of the Indaba team now visiting the diocese of El Camino Real. I'd like to bring you the greetings of a Church of St Jude in my diocese, but, despite having 390 churches, I don't think we have a St Jude – I'm sorry about that. Some fairly obscure English saints – Kenelm, Arilda, Swithun, Edward and Oswald – but no Jude!

I love Thomas Cranmer's collect for this feast, written for the First English Prayer Book in 1549. 'O almighty God, who hast knit together thine elect into one communion and fellowship in the mystical body of Christ thy Son our Lord.' 'Knit together in one communion and fellowship' – isn't that a beautiful phrase? The prayer goes on to say that we will come to those ineffable joys that God has promised to those who love him.

'Knit together in one communion and fellowship.' Well, let's unpack that a little in relation to those three readings appointed for today, from Revelation, from the First Letter of John, and from Matthew.

What's the nature of this communion and fellowship? We are given four answers. The first is that it is a great and diverse company. Revelation says:

There was a great multitude that no one could count, from every nation, from all tribes and peoples and languages ... (Rev. 7.9)

You can never narrow down the communion of saints to people like yourself. It's always stretching the boundaries of inclusion to encompass more people, some of whom look and speak and act very differently from you.

Second, the communion of saints is a family. The Letter of John reminds us of that when it says:

Beloved, we are God's children now; what we will be has not yet been revealed. (1 John 3.2)

And among those who are blessed in the teaching of Jesus in Matthew are the ones – the peacemakers – who will be called 'the children of God'. Children of God, a family with a God we call 'Father'. That's the communion of saints.

A great and diverse company, a family. Third, a worshipping community. This great and diverse company of God's family worships. That's what the Revelation reading is emphasizing:

They cried out in a loud voice, saying, 'Salvation belongs to our God who is seated on the throne, and to the Lamb!' ... and they fell on their faces before the throne and worshipped God, singing, 'Amen! Blessing and glory and wisdom and thanksgiving and honour and power and might be to our God for ever and ever!' (Rev. 7.10–12)

Worship God is what we do before all else in the communion of saints.

A great and diverse company, a family, a worshipping community. Fourth – here we need to go to the Gospel. As members of the communion of saints we are citizens of the kingdom of heaven. Did you notice in the Beatitudes the only outcome mentioned twice is being part of the kingdom of heaven?

Blessed are the poor in spirit, for theirs is the kingdom of heaven ... Blessed are those who are persecuted for righteousness' sake, for theirs is the kingdom of heaven. (Matt. 5.3–10)

We who follow Jesus belong with the angels and the saints, drawn into the experience of, the citizenship of, heaven.

So that's the description. That's what the communion of saints is. A great and diverse company, a family, a worshipping community, citizens of heaven. But what does that mean for our witness as Church? It is not actually very difficult to say, though some of it is quite challenging to achieve.

If it is a great and diverse company, we need to recognize and work for inclusivity. 'Every tribe, nation, people, language' is a way of saying everyone you can think of, all the people you would expect; but some others too, some you are not so sure you wanted to include. But God includes them and so does Jesus who died for them all. The Church is at its most wonderful when people of every class, culture and ethnic background coexist side by side and delight in one another. We know that *in theory*. In practice, our congregations, despite our best efforts, can turn out to be companies of the like-minded, all the people around us rather like ourselves. The Episcopal Church has led the way in challenging some sorts of exclusivity – in relation to the role of women in ministry, in relation to the acceptance of gay and lesbian people, for instance. The Church of England can learn much from you in this regard. But there are other more subtle elements of exclusivity we all have to work at if we really want to encompass people of every tribe, nation, people and language.

If the Church is to be a family – the children of God – we need to work for deep loving relationships with one another. Inclusivity can be fairly cold and formal. Being children of God together in one family means both the love and intimacy that we look for in the best of family life, and the struggles to achieve it and hold it that are sometimes part of the dynamic of family life – which is not always sweetness and light. Learning to trust one another, learning to hold together when actions threaten to separate, learning to love one another deeply. That's the task.

If we are to be a worshipping community, we need to ensure that, alongside our love for one another – indeed, prior even to our loving of one another – is our love for God, our focus on God in all God's beauty, holiness, mystery and loveliness. It can be too easy for the Church to find itself so engaged at the horizontal level, relating people to one another, that the vertical, the priority of worshipping God, takes second place. That is not the way it is as Revelation describes the life of heaven. Worship has absolutely central place – all eyes and hearts fixed on God and on the Lamb; that is, on Jesus. What we are doing now matters deeply and fundamentally.

And if we are citizens of heaven, then we have a calling, a duty, to strive with God to create the kingdom of heaven on earth. For the kingdom that Jesus Christ inaugurates is not intended only for some future world, but for here and for now – the values of the kingdom of heaven established on the earth. 'Your kingdom come on earth as it is in heaven', as we shall pray a little later. It is, of course, a kingdom of the Beatitudes, a kingdom of the poor in spirit, the mourners, the meek, the ones who hunger and thirst for righteousness, the pure in heart, the persecuted and the peacemakers. And citizens of heaven are engaged in establishing it on the earth.

I believe our partnership and the Indaba process in which we are engaged contribute significantly to these objectives. The partnership, now nearly three years old, El Camino Real, Western Tanganyika and Gloucester, has been and will continue to be a significant setting for exploring inclusiveness in the Church, especially in relation to sexuality, for learning to trust and to love, and to have a sense of family across some challenging divides in the Anglican Communion and for working for the kingdom of heaven on earth – not least through pursuit of the Millennium Development Goals. And in all our meetings, encounter with the living God, worship and the study of the Scriptures has been our starting point, one to which we have kept returning. And the Indaba conversations, in which we are now engaged at the request of the Communion, are an intensifying of those partnership objectives. It's a privilege to be engaged with them.

So, whether in the worldwide Church, or in our partnership, or in each church community including your own, we aim high. We want to sense ourselves part of that communion and fellowship. But, being realistic, we do not live in a perfect Church, any more than we live in a perfect world. Sometimes, in the words from Revelation, we can sense ourselves coming 'through a great ordeal' or, in the words of the Beatitudes, we can be among those who mourn, who hunger and thirst for righteousness but do not find it, those who are persecuted, those who are reviled.

For the kingdom of heaven, despite our best efforts, only seems to break out on earth in glimpses, establishes itself only in pockets. You find it among the poor in spirit, the meek, the pure in heart and the peacemakers. It needs the activity of a gracious God to advance the mission. And a gracious God is exactly what we have. This is the God of whom Revelation speaks:

The one who is seated on the throne will shelter them. They will hunger no more, and thirst no more; the sun will not strike them, nor any scorching heat; for the Lamb at the centre of the throne will be their shepherd, and he will guide them to springs of the water of life, and God will wipe away every tear from their eyes. (Rev. 7.15–17)

This is the God who shelters, who leads to the water of life (not least in baptism), who feeds (here in the Eucharist), who shepherds – Jesus, the Lamb turned Shepherd.

And that's for now, not for later. 'We are God's children now. What we will be has not yet been revealed.' But we have some clues about the ineffable joys that await us, the 'ineffable joys' of the collect. We will see God as he is – the Letter of John tells us that. We will be part of an even greater multitude – Revelation assures us of that. The tears will have been wiped away – Revelation assures us of that too. But the key thing is, although that may not all be complete, that it has begun – we are already knit together:

A great and diverse company.
A family.
A worshipping community.
Citizens of heaven.

Knit together in one communion and fellowship in the mystical body of Christ our Lord.

So rejoice, people of God, and praise the Lord!

Remembrance Sunday

I cannot call to mind a Remembrance Sunday when it has been more difficult to know quite where to focus. Perhaps it is only for me, but it does feel that this is the year when the wars and conflicts since 1945 have come to have an equal place in the hearts of the people of this nation, an equal place with the great world wars that first gave us Remembrance Sunday and Armistice Day.

It is partly, of course, the death over the last year of a number of the last veterans of the Great War of 1914–18. It is not that we now can afford to forget that dreadful waste of human life; we will be foolish if we ever do that. But no longer are there those for whom that war still produces raw grief and personal loss. To that extent, we move on.

But it is chiefly, of course, because of Afghanistan. We have had other conflicts since 1945, some with dramatic loss of life, as in the Falklands. But a short sharp conflict, such as the Falklands, or even to some extent the major campaigns in Iraq, do not give us, week after week, month after month, news of heroism, news of casualties, news of fatalities, and the bringing home of the bodies of those who have died in the cause of trying to bring political stability and to establish international peace. This has been the year of poignant images of families receiving back their dead, of young widows gripped by grief and yet showing a dignity in bereavement that has both won our admiration and also drawn us into their sense of loss. This Remembrance Sunday seems to be as much about the conflicts in which we are engaged now, and the people who fight in them, as about the wars we want to call to mind and the people who fought in them.

We do well to acknowledge that shift. It may in time, perhaps in quite a short time, lead us to re-evaluate just what we do and how we do it on Remembrance Sunday, because whatever is uppermost in our hearts today, we clothe our remembrance in the words and the rituals that came from the need of a nation to commemorate its dead 90 years ago. And the way we do it still speaks powerfully to some (to me certainly), but perhaps we need a way of drawing in a generation that may need to express its gratitude and its grief in a different way. Remembrance Sunday must involve the young, and not just the young who belong to organizations that wear uniforms.

There is, of course, a danger in this new emphasis. It is that those who fought in the Second World War and those who were injured or bereaved then, some of whom are still with us, will feel that we have forgotten that there was not one great world war of the twentieth century, but two. It was a different sort of war. Many members of the armed forces died, though not as many as in the first war. But the cities of the nations at war and the civilian populations suffered a good deal more. Dreadful atrocities on an unprecedented scale were part of it, principally the obscenity of the Holocaust. It was not simply a war between proud empires, but a war to halt the march of an evil regime. I do not want Afghanistan, because it grips us today, to diminish in our minds the need today to hold in our memory, with affection and honour, those who fought between 1939 and 1945, and particularly among them those who died. Today we will remember them.

I've talked a little about how we remember and how that is changing. I want to explore that just a little more, because we have *two* days of remembering and they have different styles of remembering.

Armistice Day, always 11 November, whatever day of the week, calling us back to the signing of the Armistice 91 years ago at 11 o'clock on the 11th day of the 11th month, and Remembrance Sunday, a variable date, but always the Sunday nearest 11 November. Most years they do not coincide. Both are important, but they are not the same. Each has its emphasis. Each has something to teach us and a response to draw from us. Whereas, after the Great War of 1914–18, the focusing of the nation's memory on the loss of life of war was always on 11 November, whatever the day of the week, after the Second World War the decision was taken to focus on the nearest Sunday to the 11th and to name it Remembrance Sunday. And for decades the 11th day, though not the 11th hour, was neglected except in those rare years when the 11th was a Sunday. And then came the successful campaign by the Royal British Legion to restore Armistice Day, not as a substitute, but as an additional observance.

What Armistice Day gives us when, on a busy weekday, people stop for two minutes of silence, in their workplace, in their school, in the shops, in their cars, is something rather private and personal. There are no communal words; there are no prayers. Although there is a kind of fellowship that comes from being silent together, there is a sense that each has his or her own thoughts. Personal and private, none the worse for that and, because no words are spoken, able to unite in a common silence people of many faiths and none, many ideologies and none, peace-campaigners, old soldiers and war protesters, all together.

The hope has to be that, in many human hearts, that silence moves beyond remembrance, where it properly starts, to thoughts of how we are to ensure that world war never happens again and how we can end the violence and devastation that mars regions of our world today and draws us in, as in Iraq and Afghanistan. The hope has to be that people, with their private thoughts, will ask, 'How can there be peace on earth unless it begins with me?' The individual has to reflect on how to make a difference, how to be an instrument of peace. We need that to happen, for we need people to be challenged to play their own individual and personal part in establishing peace and justice and freedom on the earth, even if all they can do is to counter the negative tendencies in their own hearts and in their own communities. 'Let there be peace on earth and let it begin with me.' 'Blessed are the peacemakers', said Jesus, 'for theirs is the kingdom of God.'

So was Remembrance Sunday a mistaken development? Should we return to a single ceremony on the 11th, recognizing that, to be honest, everything coming to a standstill on Monday morning, or Tuesday or Wednesday, or Thursday or Friday and, as far as the shops are concerned, Saturday, is better? No, it was not mistaken, for Remembrance Sunday celebrates community and Remembrance Sunday brings in God.

Remembrance Sunday brings people together. Quite extraordinarily, it might seem, in many places it brings more people together in these early years of the twenty-first century than for a long time. Perhaps that is partly because, though the two great world wars withdraw somewhat into history, modern means of communication make us more aware of the conflicts of our own time and the loss of life, of service personnel and civilian population, in them all. We are more aware of losses like that, whether in Afghanistan or Iraq or elsewhere, whether of forces personnel from Gloucestershire or from further afield, than we used to be. And that is partly why we want to come together. But there is also, in the face of the folly of war and the need to face down fanaticism and oppression, a need to come together to find a common language and to act some shared rituals that enable us to express a communal commitment to the creation of a better world. I will never overcome alone. But together, whole communities, whole nations, with a passion for justice, for reconciliation, for peace, can overcome. Standing together at war memorials and cenotaphs, coming together in churches and cathedrals and, perhaps, in mosques and temples, expresses that.

For Remembrance Sunday celebrates community and Remembrance Sunday brings in God. And that seems to me to be very important and it is what our Armistice Day fails to do. In its wordless silent tribute it is a privatized and secular commemoration. And that's all right, as far as it goes. But the genius of Remembrance Sunday is that it places our remembering within the context of prayer and our reflecting within discourse about God.

For people of faith, to place our remembering within the context of prayer is crucial. We entrust the dead to a loving and merciful God. 'Rest eternal grant to them, O Lord, and let light perpetual shine upon them', we pray. We see their sacrifice in relation to the supreme sacrifice of the Lord Jesus Christ upon the cross. We make our prayers for peace through Christ who is our peace and whose death has reconciled us to the Father. To envelop the silence in prayer is to lift it to a higher plane, to make the connection between our need and the grace of God.

'Come, let us go up to the mountain of the Lord, that he may teach us his ways and that we may walk in his paths', wrote the prophet Micah in the words we have heard this afternoon. And that, in a sense, is what we are doing in this service. 'Come,' we say to one another, when the wreath-laying is done, 'let us go to the place of the Lord, let us go to the cathedral, that God may teach us his ways and that we may walk in his paths.' If our longings for peace, whether private thoughts or shared words, are no more than our own longings, they are, to be honest, likely to be futile. But, if we can harness our own longings to the passion of God for his world, his longings, which are deeper and infinitely more dependable than our own, if we can but learn his ways and walk in his paths, then, yes, we might see more peace, more justice, more freedom in our world. But we need to turn to God and not to live and work in our own strength alone.

What is it that people are willing to die for in war? The answer to that is much more complex than is sometimes recognized. Whether 70 years ago in Europe or only days ago in Afghanistan, it is much more complex than 'for Queen and country'. It is probably also over-simplistic to say 'for

Christian civilization'. But, somewhere in the complexity of a more honest answer, I hope it's true, I believe it's true, that part of what we defend, both through armed conflict when we are driven to it, and more often through more peaceful means when they are available to us, is a freedom to put our trust in a gracious God, our helper and defender, the one who longs for perfect fulfilment for all his children and for his whole creation. And we need a Remembrance Sunday to renew our trust in him, without whom our remembering could be futile. Individual silent remembering is not sufficient. We need to be able to say, with Isaac Watts, 'O God, our help in ages past, our hope for years to come.'

So, brothers and sisters, give thanks that there is an Armistice Day, the 11th of November, with its call to each one of us, individually, privately, silently, to remember and to pledge ourselves, each one, to be a peacemaker. But give thanks that this is Remembrance Sunday, that binds us together, gives a shared sense of both grief and pride, invites us to make common cause, puts our remembering into a religious context of prayer and helps us see that it is as we walk in God's paths and let him teach us his ways that we shall discover how to bring peace and justice on the earth.

Feast of Christ the King

The twentieth century, and the late twentieth century at that, was drawn to the picture of Jesus Christ as king, and the arrival of the twenty-first century has not diminished that. Of course it is not new, but it is a renewed emphasis. Evangelical Christians sing in their songs:

He is the king of creation.
Jesus, we enthrone you, we proclaim you as our king.
Magnify, come glorify, Christ Jesus the king.
Majesty, worship his majesty, Jesus who died, now glorified,
King of all kings.

And it is not restricted to songs of a particular type. George Bell's 'Christ is the king' and Michael Saward's 'Christ triumphant, ever reigning' are among the most popular modern hymns. 'Christ the King' was a particularly favourite church dedication – supremely, of course, the metropolitan cathedral in Liverpool. And, as for the Feast of Christ the King, whereas most feast days have their origin in the first Christian millennium, the Feast of Christ the King first enters the calendar of the Roman Catholic Church in 1925, under the influence of Pope Pius XI, and the calendar of the Church of England in 1997.

Now giving glory to Jesus Christ as king is not new; it's true to Scripture. But giving it particular prominence has been, as you can see, a recent emphasis. It somehow meets a contemporary need. And I wonder why?

Particularly, I wonder why because Jesus himself was so

reluctant to allow the word 'king' to be attached to him. Choosing Gospel readings for the Feast of Christ the King must have been a problem for those who devise lectionaries, for never once does Jesus call himself a king. He talks a lot about the kingdom, and the penitent thief echoes what we so often hear from Jesus as he asks, 'Jesus, remember me when you come into your kingdom.' And most of the New Testament shares the reluctance of Jesus about this title. Paul, for instance, in the Letter to the Colossians speaks of him as 'the image of the invisible God, the firstborn of all creation, the head of the body, the beginning, the firstborn from the dead'. 'In Christ the fullness of God was pleased to dwell.' Everything except Jesus as king.

So perhaps today should be called the Feast of Jesus the non-king. Maybe that is going too far. But the key message is this. If Jesus is a king, he is such an entirely different kind of king from anything else you may have met that you have got to rethink entirely and fundamentally the picture you have of what a king might be.

So what do we mean when we speak, however tentatively, of Jesus Christ as king?

We mean, first of all, that we place Jesus – or, more accurately, we believe that God has placed Jesus – where people have always pictured only God, the Creator, the Father. People of every culture and race and age have spoken of God as a kind of king, that God is supreme, that God is enthroned, that God commands our obedience. On that, all who believe in God might agree. But the Christian says, '*Jesus* is king. All those things you say about the creator God, we say about Jesus Christ, the one who lived among us and died at our hands. He is king. He is lord.' It is Jesus, who became one of us, to whom is given power and glory, majesty and authority, who is proclaimed as king. In an age when we are more conscious than in the past of other religions and ideologies and when we, rightly, listen to the insights of other faiths, it is good that we are clear about the unique place for Christians of Jesus Christ. He is in the place of God. In that sense, he is king.

That is important for us because it enables us to see and believe something very important about Jesus. But it is also important for other reasons.

It is important because it affirms something about our humanity. Yes, it is Jesus who is uniquely king, but, yes, it is a Jesus who is one of us, our brother, as the Letter to the Hebrews puts it, in every way save sin. We live in an age when people often feel insignificant, powerless, marginalized, without value. Most of us experience that to some extent, but we know that there are many in the world who, with good reason, feel it much more than we do. This sense of the powerlessness of the individual has been particularly strong in our generation. When we celebrate Jesus as our king, we celebrate the ultimate dignity, value, honour and recognition accorded to our human race. Jesus, our brother, one of us, he is on the throne, he is the king and, in a sense, we, part of his kingly priesthood, are up there with him. And that affirms us – and heaven knows, in this generation, we do need quite a lot of affirming much of the time.

We celebrate Jesus as king because it underlines for us a truth about him. We celebrate Jesus as king because it affirms the dignity of our humanity. And, third, we celebrate Jesus as king because it tells us something important about suffering.

The one who is king is the one who was humiliated, the one to whom soldiers bowed down in mockery – 'Hail, king of the Jews!' – only minutes away from that gospel exchange between Jesus and Pilate about the nature of his kingdom. Jesus is the one on whose brow was pressed the cruel crown of thorns. Jesus is the one whose inscription as he died was 'The King of the Jews'. Jesus is the one whom the penitent thief acknowledged as having a kingdom to which he was going:

Jesus, remember me when you come into your kingdom.
The head that once was crowned with thorns in crowned
with glory now.
A royal diadem adorns the mighty victor's brow.

When we celebrate *Jesus* as king, we proclaim that lovely, but paradoxical, truth that suffering triumphs, for the one on the throne still has the scars. And that, if we understand it properly, is an important corrective to a superficial kind of triumphalism that celebrates Christ as king as if he were a great hero walking tall, wishing on Jesus images of power and authority that ill become him.

Yes, Christ is the king, but it is a kingship like no other, and the only crown is the crown of thorns. We need always to be wary of a religion that claims the victory, but loses sight of the victim on the cross. Christ is the king, but in him kingship is transformed, turned on its head. The paradox is that the throne is the cross, and we claim authority and power for him who let it all slip away, drained himself of it, and claimed his kingdom only with his dying breath. And we mustn't lose sight of that sort of theological truth when, with uplifted hearts, we celebrate with joy and confidence, as we do on this feast day, that Jesus is our king and that he is crowned with many crowns.

Again, this is a message that our own age wants to hear, for the twentieth century was a century of unparalleled violence and killing and thus of suffering. For many, the twentieth century was the century when faith was lost. How could there be a God of justice and compassion for a world of Hiroshima, Auschwitz and AIDS? But, for others, for Christians, there has been an answer to that. There is such a God, but he reigns from the throne of the cross, with a suffering that is redemptive.

I come back again and again to a profound and lovely poem written by that remarkable priest of the last century, W. H. Vanstone. He included it in his book *Love's Endeavour, Love's Expense*. Indeed, the book takes its title from the poem. The key stanza for today is this:

> *Thou art God; no monarch thou*
> *throned in easy state to reign;*
> *thou art God, who arms of love*
> *aching, spent, the world sustain.*

Christ is a new kind of king.

'Truly I tell you,' says Jesus to the penitent thief, 'today you will be with me in paradise.' This is another of those wonderful subversive inclusive welcomes we expect from God and hear on the lips of Jesus. 'Come to me,' is always his invitation. But here he uses the word 'paradise'. 'Remember me in your kingdom'. 'Today you will be with me in paradise.'

You find 'paradise' only four times in the Bible. Indeed, you need the Old Testament in Greek, rather than Hebrew, to find even four. Paul uses it once in 2 Corinthians; Jesus uses it here. Otherwise it is a beginning and end word, for it is there at the beginning in Genesis 2, a garden, more a parkland, God plants in paradise, and it's there at the end in Revelation 2, the paradise of God, with its picture of the consummation of all things. And Jesus chooses to use it at this moment as he hangs upon the cross. And, if he, Jesus, is the alpha and the omega, the beginning and the end, this is the moment where his authority is focused. The paradise moment offering life, to which all will look from the beginning of creation and to which all will look back from the end of time, is when Jesus offers forgiveness and welcome from the cross, to the penitent thief, but in a sense to each one of us. And it is that picture of the one crowned with thorns holding out the promise of paradise that defines more than any other what this new kind of kingship at the heart of a new kind of kingdom might be.

Protecting the Holy Places

National Association of Diocesan Advisers in Women's Ministry Conference

My sisters (my brothers), I need to begin with gratitude. Inasmuch as I can speak for my brother bishops (and you will know that I don't always speak for them all or they for me), I want to thank you for your ministry. The women whose ministry you affirm and support take opportunities, I am sure, to thank you. The bishops who appoint you, the bishops whom you sometimes affirm, sometimes challenge, may not always be as quick to express their thanks. But your ministry of both encouragement and challenge is a vital one. You have made a difference and you will continue to make a difference and, in so doing, will bring nearer the day not just when women can be bishops, but when gender is not an issue in the Church of England. And, if I cannot speak entirely for all the bishops, I can speak for myself. Deeply and sincerely I honour the office of dean of women clergy or adviser for women's ministry and thank you for the wisdom, patience and resilience with which you fill that office. Thank you.

I would, of course, like to be able to confirm for you, as we meet here in Yorkshire, that the fourth-century St Helena was what, in these days when women are never girls, is still called a 'Yorkshire lass'. I'm told they believe that round here on the slight evidence that it was here in Yorkshire that her son, Constantine, was declared emperor, not far away in the city of York. Even in medieval England they didn't claim she came from Yorkshire, though Geoffrey of Monmouth claimed she came from Colchester. The truth is that she was probably born at Drepanum in Bithynia around the year 250, her father an inn-keeper, but she the wife of an emperor, though a divorced wife, and later the mother of Constantine. She became a Christian in 312, already a woman in her sixties, while her son Constantine, for all that we regard him as the first Christian emperor, remained a catechumen until his deathbed. Helena, by all accounts, was devout and generous both in the building of churches and religious houses and in the care of the poor. She was indeed a holy woman.

And I'd love to confirm for you also that she found the true cross or at least some of it, and some fourth-century writers, including Ambrose, believed she did. There are many and wonderful accounts of how this discovery was made and authenticated and Helena's role is central to them. I fear they are legendary; no evidence supports them. I do not doubt that Helena venerated the cross, meditated on its mysterious beauty, was drawn by its love and its power, understood both its scandal and its glory, but probably just like you or I do, reflecting on the Scriptures, drawing near to Jesus in his passion, fixing our eyes maybe on a cross or crucifix or icon that has become dear to us.

But our calendar is wise in describing Helena as the 'Protector of the Holy Places' because that is authentic and not unconnected to the exaltation of the holy cross. In 326, when relatively old, well into her seventies, Helena visited the Holy Land, to see that Constantine's instructions in relation to the holy sites were carried out. The terrace and temple of Venus were to be removed, laying bare the sites of Golgotha and the holy sepulchre. Basilicas were to be built on that site and on the site of the Mount of Olives. But before that Helena established a basilica at Bethlehem on the site, as was believed, of the Lord's birth. Helena spent most of her time in the Holy Land liberating prisoners, helping orphans and the needy, endowing convents, making gifts to all sorts of individuals and towns and overseeing the erection of shrines. She is said to have lived humbly in a convent where she did the housework. (Sounds like women's ministry – a full diary, but still having to fit in the housework!) That's where she died, around the year 329. But she was, above all else, the restorer and protector of the holy places.

How can that relate to us, and in particular to you and to all those women whom God has called to be deacons and priests and bishops in the Church today? It seems to me that you also are to be the protector of the holy places, but these will be the spiritual holy places that are ever in need of protection, the spiritual holy places that can be lost to us if there are none to protect them and to invite others in to share their mystery and their beauty. And still they are the spiritual holy places of Bethlehem, of the Mount of Olives and of the Holy Sepulchre.

The spiritual holy place of Bethlehem, the place where a woman lay down in the straw, with perhaps only a carpenter for a midwife, and there brought to birth her child, with blood and pain and fear, and then with a joy she maybe years later told her son about, for he seemed to know something of how that could be. In what remains still a very male world, in a Church still horribly patriarchal, the spiritual holy place of birth witnesses to a world that only women really understand and men can be embarrassed even to talk about, a world of messiness and blood and milk and deep emotions, of labour pains, of mothering, of intimacy. Janet Morley, of course, writes about it powerfully, yet the liturgical world still fears it and keeps it at bay:

O Eternal Wisdom, we praise you and give you thanks, because you emptied yourself of power and became foolishness for our sake: for on this (Christmas) night you were delivered as one of us, a baby needy and naked, wrapped in a woman's blood.

God our mother, you hold our life within you, nourish us at your breast, and teach us to walk alone. Help us to receive your tenderness.

Protect the holy place of birth, of Bethlehem, as a truth that needs to be part of our spirituality, part of the truth we encounter, a place into which we can invite those who want to draw close to God in God's mystery and beauty. And do not keep it a secret for the women. Invite the men also to meet God in this mystery and this beauty that can enlarge their hearts. Together let us build a spiritual basilica for this holy truth.

The spiritual holy place of the Mount of Olives, the place where the son of Mary experienced fear and loneliness and utter vulnerability. Let down by his uncomprehending friends who were apparently unable to sense his crisis (men of course!), he kneels alone and prays, with sweat and tears, like drops of blood, with a wonderful honesty that God will take away what so frightens and appals him. Here is a man open and vulnerable, intimate with his God and in the end accepting of how it must be.

We moved some way in the theology of the twentieth century away from the impassibility of God. In response to Hiroshima, Auschwitz and other tragedies of that violent century, people could no longer make sense of a God unaffected by the travails of his world, and theologians like Moltmann, Rosemary Haughton and Vanstone introduced us to a vulnerable God. And women, embracing that kind of language more naturally than men, have made that kind of language more commonplace in theology and liturgy and spirituality. And yet, although we are made in the image of the Creator, we seem within the Church to more easily attribute vulnerability to God than to accept it in ourselves and to see it as part of the divine nature implanted within us. The Church does not do vulnerability. The Church does not begin to know how to do self-emptying. Yet, of course, unless and until we do, we cannot be filled anew with the mystery and the beauty of God. And unless and until we do we shall be keeping from us something utterly liberating and life-giving.

Protect the holy place of vulnerability, of Gethsemane on the Mount of Olives, as a truth that needs to be part of our spirituality, part of the truth we encounter, a place into which we can invite those who want to draw close to God in God's mystery and beauty. And do not keep it a secret for the women. Invite the men also to meet God in this mystery and this beauty that can enlarge their hearts. Together let us build a spiritual basilica for this holy truth.

The spiritual holy place of the Holy Sepulchre, the place where a tomb was left empty, grave clothes abandoned, and a woman was reunited with the man she loved in such a way that it was her resurrection almost as much as his. 'Mary!' 'Rabboni!' We cannot know why it was that it was to the women that Jesus first appeared, and in particular to Mary, first witness to the risen Lord, apostle of the apostles, as they say in the East, without perhaps understanding what that might mean for Christian ministry. We cannot know *why*, but we know it was like that. It was the women who understood resurrection. Perhaps they, Mary Magdalene, Mary the Lord's mother, the ones who prepared his body for burial, perhaps they were the ones who had got as close as any to dying with him and so understood what it was to be raised with him.

Of course, the holy place is not in the end the sepulchre. The tomb had served its purpose, given his body a place to wait, but it remained the place of death. But, just before we leave it, it has its own message for us. It is a message about waiting, waiting with longing, waiting with patience, waiting for something we know will come, but, O, what long delay! Like the woman who waits for her labour to begin, like the mother who watches at the bedside of a sick child, like the women of the Church who wait for the affirmation and justice of the threefold ministry open to all, faith sometimes asks of us that we wait, patiently or impatiently (for both have their place), and to know that sometimes, as R. S. Thomas put it, 'the meaning is in the waiting'. So I think perhaps there is a spiritual holy place of the sepulchre, of waiting.

But only till it turns into the spiritual holy place of resurrection. It is, of course, a spiritual holy place in human minds and hearts and bodies. The spiritual holy place of resurrection. It was the women who spoke of it first and, though we all speak of it today, perhaps the voice of women still has something distinctive to say – like Mary who met Jesus in the garden and knew herself risen too, like his mother who, having stood at the cross, was there in the upper room among those who had encountered the risen Lord and waited in prayer for the coming of the Spirit.

Protect the holy place of waiting and of resurrection, of the Holy Sepulchre and of the meeting with the risen Lord, as a truth that needs to be part of our spirituality, part of the truth we encounter, a place into which we can invite those who want to draw close to God in God's mystery and beauty. And do not keep it a secret for the women. Tell the men just as Jesus told Mary to tell the men. Invite the men also to meet God in this mystery and this beauty that can enlarge their hearts. Together let us build a spiritual basilica for this holy truth.

Praise God for Helena, protector of the holy places. Praise God for her basilicas in Bethlehem, on the Mount of Olives and over the Holy Sepulchre. Rejoice, sisters (brothers), in the spiritual holy places of birth, of vulnerability, of waiting and of resurrection, and protect them with all you are worth!

Eucharist

Even youths will faint and be weary,
and the young will fall exhausted;
but those who wait for the LORD shall renew their strength,
they shall mount up with wings like eagles,
they shall run and not be weary,
they shall walk and not faint.
(Isa. 40.30–31)

That's what you read in Isaiah 40.

One of the great mistakes of the Church of England in the latter half of the twentieth century was to discount young vocations. 'Go away and experience something of life and then come back,' we said to bright, young, keen ordinands. They went away and, most of them, didn't come back. Well, perhaps some of them did – perhaps you were bright, young, keen ordinands who did come back or even never went away. And I've been profoundly grateful for the reversal of policy that Archbishop Rowan spearheaded that has meant more young ordinands. We need, all of us, to foster vocations in the young. We older people, older clergy, need to be quite humble about the fact that God can use youthful enthusiasm as effectively as he can use the experience of mature years. We need to listen to the young and to give them voice in the Church. The man who died on the cross for the world's salvation was, they reckon, 33. And there's a challenge for us – to identify and encourage vocations, young priests who can be role models for young

Christians. We need to change the culture in this as in so much else.

And yet, as Isaiah says, 'even youths will faint and be weary, and the young will fall exhausted'. And the category, fortunately a large category, who will not faint, nor be weary, is not defined by age. It is 'those who wait for the LORD [who] shall renew their strength'. It is 'those who wait for the LORD [who] shall mount up with wings like eagles ... run and not be weary ... walk and not faint'. And there are lots of people here today who come into that category. And praise the Lord for that. And there is a good word for the grey hairs and the bald heads. 'You are those,' says Jesus, 'who have stood by me in my trials.' That's a wonderful description of Christian faithful sacrificial ministry, standing by Jesus in his trials. And to those Jesus says, 'I confer on you a kingdom.' And, though the language of reward is not the one we speak, what a wonderful gracious gift it is to have an assured place in the kingdom of our servant king.

Of course all of us, young and old and somewhere in between, can have found ourselves weighed down by the sheer pressure of ministry today – weighed down, but not, please God, knocked out. I say 'today', because the present age does feel to be a particular challenge, but Paul in the Second Letter to the Corinthians found much the same all those centuries ago:

We are afflicted in every way, but not crushed;
perplexed, but not driven to despair;
persecuted, but not forsaken;
struck down, but not destroyed.
(2 Cor. 4.8–9)

I fear that ministry does sometimes mean being afflicted, perplexed, persecuted, struck down. You will have found that. It is part of what we accept for the love of Christ. But I pray we are not often crushed or driven to despair or forsaken, never destroyed. For Paul also says that we are to be 'transformed into the image of Christ'. And the image of Christ that the Gospels give us is of one who learns to live creatively through all the experiences of life, good and evil. He is not crushed by life, nor, in a sense, does he rise above it as if it cannot touch him. No, he lives creatively through it. That's what we see when we engage with him through the stages of his passion. And bit by bit, and sometimes through big leaps, we are, in Paul's words, 'transformed into the image of Christ'.

Do you remember the wonderful story of the anointing of David, where all the sons of Jesse are paraded before the prophet, and the salutary words that we need to take to heart? Samuel needs to explain why Eliab, Abinadab, Shammah and the others will not do. It is, he says, because:

> The LORD does not see as mortals see;
> they look on the outward appearance,
> but the LORD looks on the heart.
> (1 Sam. 16.7)

That could be a solemn warning if our religion is one of outward appearance, rather than one of inner commitment. But I hope that it is, rather, an encouragement. For, though our ministry may sometimes seem to fail and falter and our effectiveness often seems in doubt, if the Lord looks to our heart he will, please God, find love for him, love for his Church, love for his people.

And we can do that in a number of ways. Here are five, each one ever so briefly.

First, we can seek to know ourselves, to stop kidding ourselves, to identify our strengths and our weaknesses, to rejoice in the strengths and to face the weaknesses honestly, secure in the knowledge that God knows us better than we know ourselves and loves us, each one of us a beloved son or daughter. Know yourself. We cannot be much help to others until we have recognized our need of help. We cannot expect others to open their hearts to us if we have never found the words to share the secrets of our hearts with another. Know yourself. Know yourself loved.

Second, we can wait upon the Lord. Remember, it is those who wait upon the Lord who will renew their strength. It is those who wait upon the Lord who will run and not be weary, will walk and not faint. And waiting upon the Lord quite simply means giving priority to prayer and to worship. Not to leading worship, though that is a wonderful privilege that can bring us deeply into the presence of God. But, whether we are leading the community or kneeling alone in a church or having a quiet time at home, we need to be men and women of prayer and worshippers with the angels and the saints. There are those who have lost the art, the practice, of prayer. Without prayer our hearts grow cold and our faith in God disintegrates, though, thank God, not his faith in us. I mean disciplined prayer, fed by Scripture and liturgy, focused, with its own dedicated time and space. 'Prayer? Oh, yes, I chatter on to God as I walk the dog' is no substitute. And, if we are not very good at praying on our own and if we need to find the stimulus of colleagues to bring the daily office alive for us, we must go and find companions, clergy or laity, even in retirement, so that the heartbeat of prayer renews our strength.

Third, we can look for healing. One of the particular dangers of the professional minister is to so adopt the role of the healer, the comforter, the absolver, that we no longer look to be healed, to be comforted, to be absolved. And, in so doing, we cut ourselves off from grace. How often we lead prayers for the sick as if we had no realization that we need to come ourselves to the physician of life. How often we pray for those in need of healing as if we were not among them. If we are to be transformed into the image of Christ, we need to look for healing. 'Ransomed, healed, restored, forgiven' – that's you and me.

Fourth, we should yearn for Christ-likeness. Being gradually conformed to Christ, embracing his pattern of living through dying and living again, is the outworking of our baptism. It is the work of a lifetime; you and I are still a work-in-progress even after all these years. Sometimes it is slow and painful work. Sometimes we seem to be going into reverse. There is a sort of spiritual snakes and ladders. But sometimes it can go forward by leaps and bounds. Sometimes, especially perhaps in Holy Week, we get inside the mind of Christ, identify with him, follow him to Calvary and find ourselves not so much standing in the shadow of the cross, but there with him, lifted up and looking out on his world with Christ-like love. Maybe we are not quite there yet. But that's where we are trying to be, for we yearn for Christ-likeness.

And, finally, we should rejoice in the Spirit:

> *The Spirit of the Lord is upon me, because he has anointed me to bring good news to the poor.* (Luke 4.18)

The Spirit is celebrated as we take bread and wine and look up to heaven and pray as we shall today:

> *We praise and bless you, loving Father, through Jesus Christ, our Lord; and as we obey his command, send your Holy Spirit, on us and on these gifts that broken bread and wine outpoured may be for us the body and blood of your dear Son.* (Eucharistic Prayer E)

The Spirit is the Life-giver. The Spirit has been given to each one of us in our baptism. The Spirit has been given to each of us for our particular calling. 'Send down the Holy Spirit upon your servant for the office and work of a priest in your Church,' the bishop prays when ordaining new presbyters. The Spirit is renewed within us, giving us the gifts we need, whenever we open our hearts, whenever we share in this sacrament. Remember those words of Paul to Timothy:

> *I remind you to rekindle the gift of God that is within you through the laying on of my hands; for God did not give us*

a spirit of cowardice, but rather a spirit of power and of love and of self-discipline. (2 Tim. 1.6)

I do believe in the grace of orders. I believe even more in the grace of our Lord Jesus Christ, and the love of God, and the fellowship of the Holy Spirit.

So, brothers and sisters, do not be weighed down, but be transformed into the image of Christ. When the Lord looks into your heart may he see that you know yourself, that you wait upon him, that you look for healing, that you yearn for Christ-likeness, that you rejoice in the Spirit.

Those who wait for the Lord *shall renew their strength,*
they shall mount up with wings like eagles,
they shall run and not be weary,
they shall walk and not faint.
(Isa. 40.31)

Sermon at Bishop Michael's funeral

Very Revd David Hoyle, Dean of Bristol

I arrived a bit late. My first sight of Michael Perham was in April 2004; the day of the Confirmation of his Election as Bishop of Gloucester. The final hymn was *Ye choirs of new Jerusalem*. We will come back to the *choirs of new Jerusalem*.

I have two abiding memories of that evening in St Mary le Bow. The first was the sight and sound of the Proctor of the College of Canons using the word *porrect* and saying *Madam, I exhibit my proxy*. The second memory is seeing Michael stand in front of Archbishop Rowan, who spoke to him of what it might be to *take risks for God*. Michael was always eager for the task, but as he stood alone that day, I glimpsed the immensity of the burden he carried for us and for God.

One of his admirers calls Michael *fab-bishop* which is one way of measuring him. But he wasn't a very *big* bishop. He succeeded David Bentley who was seven foot in a mitre. Michael told me that, as he left the cathedral on the day his ministry here began, he heard one Gloucestershire matron say to another, 'We don't get much for our money do we?'

She got that wrong.

Another memory of that glorious day when he first came to this cathedral. I was a member of Chapter, that involved one of those liturgical journeys that were such a feature of his ministry. With Michael's liturgies you got notes *and* a map. That meant that I was with him when he finally stepped into the choir, where his family was seated. That was when his four daughters got their first sight of Michael Francis, by divine permission Lord Bishop of Gloucester and, bless them, they took in the mitre and the staff and they giggled.

Which brings me to one of the most important things I need to say. Most of us here remember a Father in God, a liturgist and so on. For a privileged few Michael was husband, father, brother. The ministry we celebrate rested on the foundations that they laid. Of two things I could be certain, when I was with Michael. We would talk about church and we would talk about his family. He was so gently proud of them. What he did, they made possible. His confidence came from a home in which he was admired, teased, loved and sustained; a home in which we were all endlessly welcome. Alison, Rachel, Anna, Sarah, Mary - Michael died in the providence of God, in the hope of Easter and surrounded by your love. Exactly as he would have had it. We share only a tiny part of *your* loss and we thank you, each of you, for what you too have given us.

Now, I got this job, preaching today, on 27 September last year. Michael had been taken to hospital the night before and heard the diagnosis. Twelve hours later, I tipped up, thinking this would be a pastoral visit. I should have known better. We talked a bit about how you say the office if you do not have the books and then he said

We need to talk about my funeral. I want you to preach. I want you to preach because you will say something about me and something about God.

Note that. Michael wants us to give glory not to him, but to God today.

He has helped us. He has given us our liturgy today. He chose this and, some of it, he wrote. Our final blessing is Michael's voice, so is the Intercession. It gives glory to God. *Something about me and something about God.*

He chose this. And he yet he left me with a choice of gospel reading. He told me I must choose between two gospel readings, John 6 (which we heard) or Luke, and the Emmaus Road.

They are both Eucharistic passages. Michael was what Michael Ramsey called *a man of the Eucharist*. We are all people of the Eucharist. We have to be. In all the words and outcomes and agendas and vision statements of the church we must come *here* and do *this* because this is what Christ did for us. Michael knew that. In his *New Handbook of Pastoral Liturgy* – after a careful description of Ember Days and Advent wreaths – he went up through all the gears

> *In the eucharist ... We bring to God his world, and in our communion we taste and see how he satisfies. In the eucharist we call down the Spirit who touches and transforms, not only bread and wine, but people and relationships.* (p. 253)

The Eucharist is what Christ did and what Christ makes us. Here we have to die to live. Here we are made human and become a company. The liturgy helps that happen. So, the liturgist in Michael thought, the gospel today should be Emmaus. Emmaus, in a sense, was always his gospel.

And yet he handed me this choice.

He did that because despite his lifelong commitment to the action of breaking bread and he talked about that so well, he wanted us to remember always that it is not even the liturgy in the end that counts, but the place it takes us.

In a sermon in Oxford, eight years ago, he said this:

> *'Let the one who boasts, boast in the Lord.'* ... *We have [our] treasure in clay jars, so that it may be made clear that this extraordinary power belongs to God and does not come from us.*

This extraordinary power belongs to God. Eucharist is thanksgiving because it is a gift of God. *That* is why John 6 matters. The crowd on the hill had nothing. They were fed out of God's abundance and God's generosity. That is the point; we give thanks because we are grateful, *indebted*. Meister Eckhart said, 'If the only prayer you say is thank you it will be enough.'

Michael made the ministry of thanksgiving his own. He wrote about creation singing the Creator's praise but did not want us to think about how well we are doing when we are praising God:

It is not what they do but what God does.

This funeral had to be a Eucharist, of course it did. And Michael would have been delighted by our thanksgiving today, but Michael would want all this offered back to God who gave us this, gave us Michael.

How many clergy here heard him pray over them, as they received the cure of souls?

Receive it confidently.
Serve Christ joyfully.
Put your trust in God.
He is faithful.

We are so fascinated with ourselves and Michael always wanted us to put the book or the mirror down and lift our eyes to heaven.

And then, there is something else.

John 6 has all those crumbs, all that gathering together:

from the fragments of the five barley loaves, left by those who had eaten, they filled twelve baskets.(John 6.13)

Twelve baskets, one for each of the tribes of Israel. Not an accident, everyone is gathered in, everyone is included. God acts, we receive, and our communion creates community. Surely, that was the great theme of Michael's episcopate. He believed in church; he *so* wanted us to be church.

Liturgy, he said, was *playing at heaven*, he wanted us to be the Church that longs for and lives the Kingdom. He wanted us reconciled with one another, and diverse and inclusive. He committed to the ministry of women. He committed to the

Franciscans, understood *their* place in the richness of our life. He committed to those hard, wonderful conversations with El Camino Real and Western Tanganyika. There was the commitment to India and to Sweden. And he swept us along. I was skeptical, actually I was downright grumpy. I was sent for three days to Uppsala and came back grinning from ear to ear. Yet one more person, borne along on the tide of Michael's good grace.

Let's not forget, in all our seriousness, today that this good and gracious man *bounced* through his ministry with energy, enthusiasm and with humour. He smiled. I must remember that and I must smile more.

On his episcopal ring were the words **ut unum sint,** *that they may be one.* He brought us together for teaching and for pilgrimage, for prayer and praise. He brought us together in his home, in the cathedral, in deaneries, in synod and in meetings – he was a very good chairman.

And of course, he wanted us to be Church to share the inheritance of the saints. Michael *loved* the saints. All those collects, blessings and intercession: a hundred or so contributions to *Common Worship.* And always the saints and angels. My own favourite is the collect for Lancelot Andrewes where you hear both Michael and Bishop Andrewes:

perfect in us that which is lacking in your gifts,
of faith, to increase it,
of hope, to establish it,
of love, to kindle it,
that we may live in the light of your grace and glory.

No-one here needs me to tell them that prayer mattered to Michael. The last conversation we had, on Good Friday, was a conversation about prayer. It wasn't just that he prayed, wrote about prayer, led us in prayer… he prayed for us. He worked his way through a list of names. And he *lived* with a list of names, the names of the host of heaven.

He loved the Church, he wanted us to be Church. The clergy are not good at loving the Church. I had a brush with my confessor years ago when I grumbled about my parishioners and I got a roasting. Quite right too. For years after I had the words of the Common Prayer Ordination service on my desk:

Have always therefore printed in your remembrance, how great a treasure is committed to your charge. For they are the sheep of Christ, which he bought with his death.

Michael's legacy to us is rich in texts, but do not look for him there. Remember the man, the love of communion, the love of us, the *theological* legacy that tells us that when we step into church we enter the theatre of redemption. Here we can be what God would have us be.

In that hope and that joy he lived and died. That explains the extraordinary grace and resilience we saw in testing times. That explains the irrepressible enthusiasm, that explains the energy that never left him.

We sang *Ye choirs of new Jerusalem* that day when his election as bishop of this diocese was confirmed. I have always been inclined to think heaven is a feast. Michael knew it was a choir, the concert of praise, the harmony of lives. To that company, and that choir, we commit him in such bitter sorrow, for he was husband, father, friend. But we are grateful, for he reminds us to be church and sustain one another. And we are confident, because he knew, and we know, that God will be faithful to him.

Something about me, something about God. We can't think, or speak, of Michael without speaking of God and of his Church. In gratitude then, we commend Michael in the company of angels and saints and we commit ourselves, once more, to that full communion in which Michael lives and we hope; now and forever.